GW01605877

ENID BLYTON'S
PIXIE TALES

Enid Blyton's

PIXIE TALES

COLLINS
LONDON AND GLASGOW

This Impression 1971

ISBN 0 00 163210 8

PRINTED AND MADE IN GREAT BRITAIN BY
WM. COLLINS SONS AND CO. LTD.
LONDON AND GLASGOW

CONTENTS

The Magic Silver Thread

ONCE upon a time there lived a wizard called Deep-Eyes, who had one son called Ho-Ho, a baby boy of twelve months old. Ho-Ho used to crawl about the wizard's work-room whilst Deep-Eyes was making his spells, and one day a dreadful thing happened.

Deep-Eyes was making a spell for a witch who wanted her apple trees to grow bigger and stronger. He mixed all kinds of things together, and put the mixture in a blue bowl to cool. He set it on a low table, and then took down one of his magic books to read.

The baby found the bowl and liked the look of the golden, shining water inside. He suddenly took hold of it, jerked it into the air, and spilt it all over himself! Then what a to-do there was!

Ho-Ho cried and licked the mixture that was running all down his face. It soaked his clothes, and made him shiver. The wizard shouted aloud in dismay and ran to his little son. The mother came rushing into the room, and picked him up.

"What a silly you are to stand bowls of water about!" she said to her husband, the wizard.

"It wasn't a bowl of water," said the wizard, with a groan, "it was a golden spell I had made for the witch who came to see me yesterday. Now it's all wasted!"

"A spell!" cried his wife, in dismay. "Good gracious, Baby has licked some of it! Will it do him any harm?"

"I shouldn't think so," said the wizard. "We must wait and see."

Well, for a little while the wizard and his wife saw nothing wrong with their son. He grew well, and was soon twice as big as children of his age. Everyone said what a fine boy he was, and how strong he looked.

But as he grew older, he shot up so tall, and became so broad that folk began to wonder.

"He's much too tall for his age," said one to another. "There must be a spell on him. Why, he's only five years old, and yet he's much taller than his father, Deep-Eyes."

Deep-Eyes soon knew what had happened. The spell he had made to make the witch's apple trees grow bigger and stronger was acting on his little boy, and making him grow huge. Soon the wizard and his wife were quite afraid of Ho-Ho, for he was so much bigger and stronger than they were.

So very soon he was allowed to do just as he liked, and everyone in the town tried to please him because he was so enormous. This was very bad for Ho-Ho, and he grew up selfish and unkind.

When he was twenty years old he was simply enormous. He reached up to the clouds, and his feet were as big as a large field. His voice was louder than thunder, and he ate more food than a hundred men could eat, at each meal.

Nobody knew what to do with him. The whole town had to find food for him, and if by chance he did not have enough to eat, he would stamp his great feet till houses fell to pieces and everyone shook and shivered in fear.

At last he stopped growing, but he was easily the biggest giant in the world, and the most selfish. Nobody knew what to do with Ho-Ho, for he would not work. He told everyone they must work for him, or he would smash the town to bits.

One winter it was very cold indeed, and Ho-Ho commanded the townspeople to build him a great castle. But though they tried their best they could not build one that reached to the top of the giant's head. So they decided that he would be better off in a deep cave under the earth.

"You will be warm there, Ho-Ho," they said. "The frost will not reach you, and you will be sheltered from the wind. There is not enough stone in the kingdom to build a castle big enough for you, so you must be content with a cave. We will make it very comfortable."

At first Ho-Ho wouldn't listen, and demanded his castle—but soon he began to think that he might indeed be very cosy in a deep cave, and he told the little people to find one for him.

They did not trouble to find one. They asked Deep-Eyes the Wizard to make one for them, and he brewed a very strong magic, said seven strange words, and emptied the magic on to the ground. Lo and behold, a cave opened beneath his feet large enough to hold a dozen giants in comfort.

"Ho-Ho should be very comfortable in such a large cave," said the people. The giant had his bed put there, a chair and a table, and soon made himself cosy.

"If only we could keep him there for always!" sighed the people. "But in the spring he is sure to come out again, trample on our houses, and frighten everyone till they shiver and shake."

"Couldn't we manage to tie him up?" asked Twinkles, a small pixie.

"Pooh!" said the chief man of the town, "what an idea! Who do you suppose is going to tie Ho-Ho up, I should like to know!"

"I might be able to," said Twinkles. "I could think of a plan, I'm sure."

Everyone laughed loudly at him, and he went away rather red in the face. He packed his bag and caught the train to Fiddle-Dee, the village where a great blacksmith lived. Twinkles made his way to his house, and found the clever smith hard at work.

"Could you make me a steel chain so strong that it couldn't be broken by anyone in the world?" he asked.

"Easily!" laughed the smith. "What will you pay me for it?"

"Well, I haven't any money at present," said Twinkles, "but if you really *can* make me a chain that no one can break, I shall be rich, and will pay you what you please."

The smith agreed, and at once set to work. For four weeks he laboured hard, and at the end of that time he showed Twinkles a steel chain so strong and heavy that the little pixie could not move even one link of it.

"That will never break!" said the smith, proudly. "You will have to hire fifty horses to carry it for you."

So Twinkles got fifty horses, and they dragged the great chain behind them to the town. Everyone came to see it, and Twinkles explained that he had brought it to bind Ho-Ho with, so that he would never be able to get out of his cave.

"We will pretend to Ho-Ho that it is all a game," said Twinkles. "Come along to his cave and we will see what happens."

So everyone trooped off to the cave where the giant lived.

"Ho-Ho!" cried Twinkles, peering down. "Are you as strong as you were? There are some who say that your strength is failing!"

Ho-Ho growled angrily.

"Prove me!" he said, in a rage. "I am stronger than any other giant in the world."

"Well, here is a chain that surely even *you* cannot break!" said Twinkles, and he bade the horses gallop near.

Ho-Ho took one look at it and snorted in scorn.

"You may bind me as tightly as you please with a toy-chain like that!" he said. "I shall snap it in a moment!"

This was just what Twinkles wanted. He called the strongest men of the town to him and very soon they were binding the giant tightly with the chain, and made one end fast to a great rock.

"Ha! You are bound now!" cried Twinkles, in delight. "You cannot get free, Ho-Ho!"

But the giant only smiled. He stretched himself and pulled on the great chain. Snap, snap, snap! It broke in twenty places, and Ho-Ho was free once more!

Then all the people had to pretend to be full of wonder and delight, for they were afraid to let Ho-Ho know that they really *had* wanted to bind him fast. He smiled and laughed, thinking that they were all glad at his strength.

"Bring a bigger chain still!" he said. "I'll show you what I can do! Why, I could break a chain twenty times stronger than that!"

"Oh, no you couldn't!" cried everyone. "You really couldn't, Ho-Ho!"

"Try me and see!" said the giant.

So off went Twinkles to the smith again, and told him what had happened.

"Make a chain twenty times as strong," he begged him. "Surely the giant cannot break that!"

"I am surprised he could break the other," said the smith, marvelling. "Well, I will make this new chain for you, Twinkles, but I cannot make it alone. I must get twelve other smiths to help me."

So he sent for twelve brothers of his, all famous smiths, and the thirteen set to work to make a chain stronger than had ever been seen in the world before. In three weeks it was finished, for the smiths worked all through the night as well as by day. It took a thousand great horses to drag it along, and everyone ran by the panting beasts and cheered them on.

When Ho-Ho saw the enormous chain he looked rather solemn.

"Ha, Ha!" said Twinkles, seeing him look doubtfully at the chain. "This is twenty times as strong, and you said you could easily break it! But now that you see it, you are afraid, Ho-Ho! Fancy a great giant like you, the biggest in the world, being afraid! Well, well, we will not let you try to break it, we will take it back from where we brought it."

But Ho-Ho did not like being laughed at. He took another look at the chain, and then looked at his great arms.

"You may bind me!" he said in his thunderous voice. "I am not afraid! You will see how easily I can snap your silly chain in two!"

So a hundred strong men bound him, and made one end of the chain fast to a rock. Then everyone stood back to see what would happen. Ho-Ho took a deep breath, and then tugged hard at the chain. It held! He tugged again. Alas! It flew apart in six different places, and the giant was free!

Once again the people had to pretend to marvel at him, and to be glad that he had broken the chain. Ho-Ho smiled with pleasure, for he loved people to admire him. But he made up his mind not to be bound again, in case one day he could *not* get free.

"I am tired of this chain game," he said. "I will not be bound any more!"

Then everyone knew that it was no use to try to bind the giant, and very sadly they went away. But still Twinkles did not give up hope.

"If thirteen strong smiths cannot help me, maybe one clever dwarf can get me what I want!" he thought. So he packed his bag again and took the train that ran deep underground to the caverns of the mountain dwarfs. Soon he came to where Peer-About, one of the very cleverest of the dwarfs, had his home.

Peer-About had so much knowledge inside his head, that it had grown very big, whilst his arms and legs had remained small; so he was a queer-looking little person, but kind-hearted and always willing to help anyone.

Twinkles told him all about Ho-Ho, and how he had broken the two chains.

"I suppose you can't help me?" he asked.

"I think I can," said Peer-About, after he had thought for a moment. "Stay here for a week, and I will give you something that no giant, were he as big as the world itself, could break!"

So for a week Twinkles stayed with Peer-About in his little underground cave, and watched him work. The dwarf took the queerest things and mixed them all in a pot together. He took the footfall of six tigers, a little of the arch of a rainbow, some water from a bottomless pool, and the roots of a high mountain. Many other things he took too, that Twinkles did not know, and carefully he stirred them all up together, chanting such strange words as he did so that Twinkles felt the hair standing up on his head with fright.

When the mixture was ready the dwarf put his hands into it and then drew them out again. The stuff clung to them like wet toffee, and the little dwarf wound it neatly round a pointed stick. It looked like glistening silver thread, no thicker than sewing-cotton on a reel. Peer-About wound it steadily round his stick, and at last there was nothing left in the bowl.

"Now I must put it out into the moonlight for one night," he said, "and it will be ready."

"But, Peer-About, do you really think it will be strong enough?" asked Twinkles. "Why, it looks so slender I feel I could snap it myself!"

The dwarf smiled and said nothing. All that night the stick of silver thread lay out in the moonlight, and in the morning Peer-About made it into a small, gleaming ball of thread, and gave it to Twinkles.

"No one in the world can break that," he said. "Not even I, who made it, can snap it in two!"

Twinkles thanked the dwarf, and set off back

to his own land. When he arrived there he showed his friends what he had been to fetch and they all laughed at him. They unwound the thread and pulled it—but no matter how they tugged and twisted they could not break it.

"But surely Ho-Ho will be able to snap it in a trice!" said everyone. "It is so slender and so thin. And how are we going to bind him with it? He said he would not be bound any more."

"I have an idea," said Twinkles. "It is spring-time now and Ho-Ho will expect to leave his cave and come into the sunshine again. We will bind daisies all along the thread as if it were a daisy-chain and take it to him, pretending that we wish to deck him and lead him out into the sun. Then we will bind him tightly with it, and he will not be able to move!"

"Well, we will try," said the little people, doubtfully. "But we think that Ho-Ho will easily snap such a frail thread."

Then everyone worked hard and picked hundreds of starry daisies, tying them prettily along the silver thread, so that it looked for all the world like a mile-long daisy-chain. When it was finished they went dancing and singing to the cave where Ho-Ho dwelt, as if they were full of joy at the spring-time.

Ho-Ho looked up in surprise.

"We have come to fetch you out into the sunshine, Ho-Ho," said Twinkles. "And see! We have made up a lovely daisy-chain! Will you have it round you?"

Ho-Ho put out his hand and felt the daisy-chain,

wondering if there was a strong chain hidden among the flowers. But when he felt the slender silver thread he smiled, for that was nothing, he thought.

He allowed Twinkles to wind the daisy-chain round and round him, and then the pixie deftly tied one end to the great rock inside the cave making it fast.

"Now come, Ho-Ho," he said, skipping nimbly out of the cave. "Come out into the sunshine, decked with daisies!"

Ho-Ho stood up and tried to move forward, but the silver thread held him to the rock. He tugged lightly, thinking that the daisy-chain had become entangled in something, but still he was held fast. In a temper he pulled hard, but it was of no use—he could not get away.

Then Ho-Ho knew that he had been tricked, and he roared so loudly that chimney-pots shivered on their roofs and nearly fell off. All the little folk fled away in a panic, stuffing their fingers into their ears. Ho-Ho tugged at the thread again and again, amazed that such a slender thing should hold him so tightly. The daisies fell off one by one, as the giant twisted the thread round his great fingers.

But try as he would he could not snap it. It was far stronger than either of the chains. It slid through his fingers, and he could get no grip of it.

Then he knew he was caught and he roared aloud again in rage. He stamped his enormous feet and the earth shook. He banged on the cave walls with his fists, and the roof became so shaken that it dropped huge stones on to Ho-Ho's head, and made him angrier still.

All that day and all the night the giant roared and raged, whilst the people of the town crouched in their houses, wondering what would happen to them if the thin silver thread snapped in two. Only Twinkles was unafraid, for he knew what it was made of.

Next day he went to the giant's cave and peered down into it.

"Listen to me, Ho-Ho," he said sternly. "You are bound here for ever, but it is your own fault, for you are an unkind and selfish giant, of no use to anyone. Therefore you are made a prisoner. If you are quiet and peaceful, we will feed you each day, but if you roar and rage, you will starve."

Ho-Ho listened and knew that he was defeated. He lay down quietly, and begged Twinkles to send him some food, promising to be good if only he might have something to eat.

Off went Twinkles, and soon all the people in the town had heard the great news—the biggest giant in the world was imprisoned and bound, and could never get away. How they cheered Twinkles and clapped him on the back! They gave him one hundred sacks of gold, and he at once paid the thirteen smiths who had tried so hard to make chains strong enough for Ho-Ho.

Then with the rest of the money he bought a fine little cottage, married a pretty little wife, and settled down happily ever after.

As for Ho-Ho, he is quiet enough usually—but

The daisies fell off one by one as the giant twisted the thread round his great fingers.

sometimes, when the little people bring him food he doesn't like, he gets into one of his old rages. Then he roars and bellows, stamps and kicks, and somewhere in the world there is an earthquake!

But you needn't be afraid that Ho-Ho will ever escape—the little silver thread that Peer-About the dwarf made will hold him fast until the end of the world!

The Strange Umbrella

TIPTAP the pixie lived in Apple-Tree Cottage in the very middle of Feefo Village. He had two nice little rooms, a kitchen and a bedroom, and outside the cottage was a pocket-handkerchief of a garden—very small, but quite enough for Tiptap to manage.

Now Tiptap was the only pixie in Feefo Village who did no proper work. He had ten silver shillings a week of his own, which his old Aunt Tabitha Twinkle sent him, and he just made this do nicely. It bought him bread and butter, cocoa to drink, apple tarts from Mother Buttercup's shop, and fresh eggs from the egg-woman.

Everyone else in the village had their own work to do. The egg-woman looked after her hens and sold their nice brown eggs, the balloon man sold balloons,

Mother Buttercup made lovely cakes and tarts, and the bee-woman got honey from her bees and put it into pots. Everyone did something—except Tiptap, who was the laziest little pixie in the kingdom.

Now one day Tiptap went to see his Aunt Tabitha Twinkle, and she told him she had one or two little jobs for him to do to help her.

"There's my broom that wants mending," she said. "The handle has come off. And there's the garden gate that creaks terribly. You might stop it for me. Oh, and there's my step-ladder too—something's gone wrong with it, Tiptap, and I'd be so glad if you'd see to it."

"All right," said Tiptap rather crossly. He didn't want to mend things for his aunt. He wanted to sit in her nice new hammock and swing himself in the sun.

"I'll just have a nice swing first," he thought to himself and he ran to the hammock. But, do you know, he hadn't been swinging in the sunshine for more than two minutes when he fell fast asleep!

He slept for two hours, and then he heard his aunt calling him in a very cross voice.

"Tiptap! Tiptap! Why haven't you done all I asked you to? There's the gate still creaking, the broom still broken, and the step-ladder not mended! You are a very naughty pixie."

Tiptap tumbled out of the hammock and ran to the garden shed. He took out the oil-can and ran to the gate to oil it—but he was in such a hurry that he put far too much oil down the hinges, and spilt a lot over the gate itself. He didn't trouble to rub it off with a rag, but left it there and ran to the broken broom.

Quickly he hammered a nail into the handle, and stuck the brush on. Then he looked at the stepladder. One of the rungs was unsafe, and Tiptap saw that it would need quite an hour's work to take out the bad rung and put in a nice new one.

"Bother!" said the pixie, crossly. "I can't do that! I shall just stick the old rung in again and tell Aunt Tabitha Twinkle I have mended it. She will never know."

And that is what the lazy little creature did. Then he ran to his aunt, and said: "Did you call me, Aunt Tabitha? I have done all the jobs you asked me to, you know, so you really mustn't be so cross."

"Oh, you're a good little pixie, then," said his aunt, pleased. "Come along in and have some pink jelly. It has just set nicely, and I know you're fond of it. Then I'll give you your ten shillings and you shall go home."

Tiptap sat down to eat the jelly. Just as he was finishing it, he saw his aunt's great friend, Mother Smiley-face, coming in at the gate—and oh my! She had a fine new dress on, and the oil that Tiptap had left on the gate smeared itself all over the blue silk, and *what* a mess it made!

Mother Smiley-face was very cross. She hurried up to Aunt Tabitha Twinkle and showed her what had happened.

"There's my nice new dress all ruined!" she said.

"Whatever have you been doing to your gate?"

"Oh, that's Tiptap," said Aunt Tabitha, crossly. "He didn't wipe the gate clean after oiling it, I suppose!"

"I've come to ask you if you will let me see your new bonnet," said Mother Smiley-face, wiping her dress carefully.

"Oh, certainly!" said Aunt Tabitha, pleased. "I'll fetch it for you. It's on the top of the wardrobe. Get me the step-ladder, Tiptap."

The pixie fetched the ladder, and his aunt climbed up to get her bonnet—but, oh dear me! When she stepped on the bad rung, it broke, and then she fell, clutching at the parcels on the wardrobe as she did so, so that a whole crowd of them fell on the floor in a cloud of dust.

"Oh! Oh! You wicked little pixie! You haven't mended the ladder after all!" said Aunt Tabitha, angrily. "Oh, I've hurt my knee—and look at all the mess!"

Mother Smiley-face helped Aunt Tabitha up, and then fetched the broom to sweep up the mess—but of course the handle flew off as soon as she started sweeping, because Tiptap hadn't mended it properly.

"Well, look at that!" said Aunt Tabitha, now really angry. "I asked you to do three little things for me, Tiptap, and see how you've done them! I'm ashamed of you! You don't deserve your ten shillings a week! In future you shall only have five, and I shan't give you ten again until I see that you know how to do a piece of work well."

So Tiptap was given five shillings instead of ten, and sent home in disgrace.

Each week after that only five shillings came for him instead of ten, and soon Tiptap was in rather a bad way. He could manage to feed himself on five shillings, but if he needed anything new, he had no money to buy it. When his kettle suddenly grew a hole in it, he couldn't buy another. When his spade broke, he had no money for a new one. Of course, he could have mended them if he had set to work with a will, but he was a lazy fellow, and found it much easier to borrow from other folk instead.

So when things went wrong, Tiptap ran round to his friends.

"My clock has stopped and I can't get it going again," he said to the egg-woman. "Would you lend me one of yours, please?"

The egg-woman had two clocks, so she lent Tiptap one, thinking that when the pixie had mended his own, he would give her it back. But the lazy fellow didn't bother to try and mend his, now that he had got the egg-woman's.

When his kitchen lamp broke, he ran to Mother Buttercup, who had a spare one, and begged her to lend it to him.

"I'll soon mend mine," he promised, "and then you shall have yours back, Mother Buttercup."

But, of course, he *didn't* trouble to mend his lamp, and poor Mother Buttercup had to go without her second one for weeks and weeks.

Soon Tiptap's cottage was full of things he had borrowed, and his garden shed full of things of his own that he had broken and that were waiting to be mended. But Tiptap didn't mend a single one. No—if people were kind enough to let him have things in their place, well, he would borrow and borrow and borrow!

Now one day he broke his umbrella. He looked at it, and saw that it would take him quite two hours to mend it properly.

"Oh bother!" said Tiptap. "I'll go and borrow the balloon man's. I know he has two."

So he went to the balloon man, and asked him to lend him his second umbrella, because it was raining very hard and he wanted to go out.

"I'm sorry," said the balloon man, "but I lent my old one to my cousin yesterday, and I've only got my new one left. I can't lend you that, Tiptap, because I've got to go out selling balloons, and I must have an umbrella to keep the rain off me when I sit all day at my corner."

Then Tiptap went to the bee-woman and asked her to lend him *her* umbrella. But she wouldn't.

"I've only got one, as you know very well, Tiptap," she said. "Also, I know that if I lent it to you, you wouldn't bring it back to me. You're getting a very bad name for borrowing, and you'd better stop doing it. Where's that kettle I lent you a month ago?"

Tiptap went red, said good-bye and ran out. He tried to borrow an umbrella from Gobo, the elf who lived in the next cottage, but Gobo had no umbrella at all.

"Now what am I to do?" wondered Tiptap,

turning up his coat collar, because the rain trickled down his neck. "I do want to go and see Hey-ho the gnome this morning, and I shall get so wet if I walk across the common without an umbrella!"

But since no one would lend him an umbrella, he had to start off without one. He began to walk over the common, and he felt very cross, for the rain made him wetter and wetter.

Soon he came to Dame Trips's cottage, and he wondered if *she* would lend him an umbrella. So he ran up the garden path and popped his head in at the kitchen window.

"Could you lend me an umbrella?" he asked Dame Trips, who was busy setting two cups of cocoa on a tray.

"No," said Dame Trips, "I haven't one to lend."

Tiptap ran off again—but just as he passed the front door, what should he see standing outside in the porch but a fine umbrella! Goodness, it *was* a splendid one! It was red with big yellow spots all over it, and the handle was bright green. Instead of a little spike sticking out below the umbrella part, there was a funny knob in the shape of a little face.

"There! Dame Trips said she hadn't an umbrella, and she has, all the time! She told me a story!" said Tiptap. "I've a good mind to borrow that fine umbrella just to punish her! I can easily leave it here on my way home again."

He went up to the umbrella. It certainly was a lovely one, the biggest and brightest Tiptap had ever seen. He picked it up and ran down the path with it.

When he was out of sight, he put it up over his head to keep off the rain. Ah, if Tiptap could have seen the little knob of a face at the top then! How it grinned and winked to itself!

Now the way to Hey-ho's was towards the west, and Tiptap turned his steps there—but what was his astonishment to find that he couldn't make his legs walk that way! They seemed to want to walk in the opposite direction.

Then he heard a tiny, chuckling laugh, and he wondered where it came from.

"It sounds as if it's above the umbrella somewhere," he thought, so he peeped over the edge of it and looked—and he saw that little grinning knob of a face, winking and blinking at him for all it was worth!

"Ooh!" said Tiptap, in a fright. "Ooh! This umbrella's magic! I must throw it away at once, before it does me any harm!"

He tried to fling it from him, but dear me, he couldn't let the handle go! It seemed to hold on to his hand! Tiptap tried to take his hand away, but he couldn't. The handle closed round his fingers and held him fast.

"Ooh!" said Tiptap, beginning to cry. "It *is* magic! *Now* what's going to happen!"

He hadn't long to wait before he knew, for the umbrella suddenly began to blow along towards the north-east, just as if a great wind was behind it. It pulled Tiptap along after it, and the poor little pixie found himself running fast over the common, unable to do anything else. The big red umbrella pulled him along at a tremendous pace, and Tiptap was soon out of breath—but he *couldn't* let go the handle.

"Where's it taking me to?" he wondered, the tears pouring down his cheeks in fright. "Oh dear! It can't have belonged to Dame Trips after all. It must have belonged to someone who was visiting her! Oh, why did I take it?"

At last, after taking Tiptap about five miles over hill and dale, the umbrella came to a little white house set on a hillside. On the gate was a name—"Wizard Ho-Hum's Cottage."

Then Tiptap was more afraid than ever, for he knew that the wizard would be very angry to find his umbrella taken from Dame Trips, for he would have to walk home in the rain.

The umbrella took Tiptap to the front door, and there it stayed. There didn't seem to be anyone in the house at all. Wizard Ho-Hum was out. He had gone to see his sister, Dame Trips—and my goodness, when he came out and found that someone had taken his umbrella, what a rage he was in!

"Well, I shall find the thief outside my front door, waiting for me!" he said to himself. "My umbrella will be sure to take him there! But just look at this rain! How wet I shall get!"

So he did, for the rain poured down as he went across the common. When he at last got home, he was in a fine temper. He saw the umbrella by his front door, the handle still holding fast to Tiptap's hand, and little head at the top chuckling and laughing for all it was worth.

"Ho!" he shouted, frowning angrily at Tiptap. "So *you're* the thief, are you?"

"Please, no," said Tiptap, in a small voice. "I thought it was Dame Trips's umbrella, and I just borrowed it."

"*I've* heard all about you!" said the wizard. "You're the nasty, horrid little fellow that breaks your own things and goes about borrowing other people's and never takes them back again! Well, *I* call that stealing! Yes, I do! I'll teach you to steal *my* umbrella!"

He opened his front door, took the umbrella away from Tiptap's hand, and closed it. Then he stood it in a corner, and ordered Tiptap to go in.

"Now, I want a handy-man," he said to the frightened pixie. "You can choose what you will do—either I take you to Pop-off the policeman, and tell him you stole my umbrella, or *you* can be my handy-man for six weeks, and do all my odd jobs till my other man comes back. If you try to run away, the red umbrella will come after you and catch you. Now, which will you choose?"

"P-p-p-please, I'll b-b-b-be your handy-m-m-m-man!" stammered the pixie, who couldn't bear the idea of being taken to Pop-off.

"Then make yourself useful straight away!" commanded Ho-Hum. "Take a pail and clean all the windows. Then peel some potatoes and prepare dinner for me."

Tiptap set to work. How he made those windows shine! Then he peeled the potatoes, and put a milk pudding into the oven. After that the wizard made him chop wood till his arms ached.

What a time the pixie had for the next few weeks! He was up at daybreak, and he wasn't allowed to go to bed till he had finished every single job there was to be done. He had to keep the cottage clean and tidy, cook all the meals, work in the garden, chop the wood and mend anything that got broken, for the wizard wouldn't hear of buying or borrowing fresh things.

Once Tiptap made up his mind to run away, and in the night he crept out of the cottage—but he hadn't gone very far before he heard a little chuckle behind him, and, oh my! In the moonlight what should he see but that red umbrella just behind him! It opened itself all of a sudden and the handle caught hold of Tiptap's hand. Then he was dragged all the way back to Ho-Hum's.

The wizard found him outside the front door in the morning, held tightly by the umbrella.

"Ho, so you thought you'd try to run away, did you?" he said. "For that you shall do twice as much work to-day."

But when Tiptap had been at Ho-Hum's for a month, he found that he began to *like* his work. It was fun to make the cottage shine like a new pin. It was lovely to dig in the garden in the sun. It was exciting to mend something that was broken and make it as good as new again. Really, Tiptap quite enjoyed himself, and he began to sing and whistle at his work like a blackbird in spring.

"Ah, you're beginning to see that it is a fine thing to work!" said Ho-Hum one morning. "What a nasty, lazy, good-for-nothing fellow you used to be, to be sure! See how clever your hands are, when you set them to something. Why, I shall be quite sorry to lose you to-morrow, when my old handy-man comes back."

"Is he coming back to-morrow?" asked Tiptap in dismay. "Oh! I *shall* be sorry to go! It *will* seem funny going back home with nothing to do."

"Well, since you're such a good hand at mending and making," said Ho-Hum, "why don't you make yourself the handy-man of Feefo Village? I hear there isn't one there, and I'm sure the folk would be very glad of one."

"That's a splendid idea!" said Tiptap, pleased. "Hurrah! I'll soon show everyone I'm not lazy or good-for-nothing!"

The next day Ho-Hum's old handy-man came back, and Tiptap said good-bye to the wizard, who gave him a little tie-pin in the shape of a red umbrella, to remind him never to be lazy again. Tiptap stuck it proudly into his tie and marched home.

As soon as he got to Apple-Tree Cottage, and had set it in order again, he went to his garden shed, where were all the dozens of things he had broken and put there weeks before. He set to work to mend them, and by the end of the week there were all his tools, pots and pans, and everything else as good as new. Then Tiptap took back all the things he had borrowed, thanked the people who had kindly lent them to him, and said he was sorry he had kept them so long.

"I'm going to set up as handy-man to the village," he told everyone. "Let me have anything broken or spoilt, and I'll mend it for you for a penny or two. I want to do something for my living now!"

How astonished and pleased all the people were! They let Tiptap have all their broken things and he mended them splendidly. Soon he had quite a lot of money in his purse, and wasn't he proud of it!

Then one day his Aunt Tabitha came to see him, to give him all the five shillings he hadn't had whilst he had been away.

"You shall have *ten* shillings a week again now!" she said, when she found out how hard Tiptap was working and how changed he was. But Tiptap wouldn't take a penny!

"No, thank you, Aunt Tabitha Twinkle," he said. "I've found out that it is a hundred times nicer to earn money myself than to take it from someone else for doing nothing. Please keep it yourself, or give it to the Hospital for Sick Brownies. In future I'm going to work hard and be happy."

He kept his word, and his Aunt Tabitha sent the money to the Brownie Hospital, which was very much delighted to have it. As for Tiptap, you should hear him whistle and sing as he mends pots and pans and sharpens knives. It really is lovely to listen to him. He still has his tie-pin, and he wouldn't part with it for the world!

"That was the best thing that ever happened to me!" he often says. "I'll never be sorry that strange umbrella took me away."

The Hey-Diddle Pie

IN THE end cottage of Pinniky Village lived old Dame Criss-Cross. She was just like her name, the crossest old woman that anybody had ever met. The pixies, gnomes, and elves tried to like her, but oh dear me, it was very hard work!

Just beyond her cottage the common began. It was a lovely stretch of gorse-bushes, heather, and fine, springy grass. Bluebells grew in the dells of the common, and in the autumn blackberries ripened in thousands on the brambles.

It was a lovely place for the children of the pixies and gnomes to play. They used to go there every day and shout from morning till night.

Old Dame Criss-Cross didn't like children. She hated to hear their jolly voices, and when she heard them laugh, she frowned till her forehead was nothing but wrinkles.

"Drat those children!" she said. "Why can't they go and play somewhere else!"

When a ball came rolling into her garden, the children didn't dare to fetch it, and there it had to stay. They were all afraid of Dame Criss-Cross, and even when little Silver-toes fell down and made his knee bleed, they wouldn't go to her cottage to ask for help.

One day, when Dame Criss-Cross was just walking out of her garden gate to go shopping, a crowd of pixie children came tearing round the corner and bumped right into her. Dame Criss-Cross was sent spinning and sat down with a bump. Her basket went one way and her bonnet went another.

The pixies were sorry and frightened. They hadn't meant to knock the old woman over, of course. They picked up her basket and her bonnet, and gave them to her.

"You naughty, wicked pixies!" said the old dame, shaking her stick at them. "You did that on purpose, so you did! Well, you're not to come past my cottage any more, do you hear? If you do, I'll smack you!"

The pixies said nothing, but they ran home to their parents. The only way to get to the common was past Dame Criss-Cross's cottage—and surely they might still play among the heather and the gorse!

"Of course you shall!" cried the folk of Pinniky

Village. "Don't you take any notice of Dame Criss-Cross! We'll send her a letter that will make her shiver and shake in her shoes!"

Then Trippit, the elfin schoolmaster, wrote a letter and this is what he said:

DEAR DAME CRISS-CROSS,

If you harm our children, we will come and turn you out of your cottage, and you will never be allowed to live here again. The pixies did not mean to knock you over, and they are sorry they did. They will come and play on the common each day as they always do, and if you try to stop them, we shall punish you!

When Dame Criss-Cross got that letter, how she shivered and shook! She knew quite well that if she did beat the pixies or elves, their parents would complain to the Queen, and she certainly *would* be turned out of Pinniky Village!

So she had to let the children run past her cottage as usual, and they played happily on the common all day. But the old Dame frowned and brooded, and wondered how she could revenge herself on Pinniky Village.

At last she put on her cloak and her bonnet, took her broom-stick to ride upon—for she was half a witch—and went flying away to see her old friend, Mother Grumpy. She told her all her troubles, and Mother Grumpy listened.

"Ah!" said her friend, "so you want my help, do you? Well, Dame, I've a Hey-Diddle spell here that will do just what you want! It will spirit all those pixie children away, and they will never be heard of again. And no one will know you've had anything to do with it!"

"Give it to me!" begged Dame Criss-Cross eagerly.

"You must let me have ten gold pieces," said Mother Grumpy. "It is not a cheap spell."

Dame Criss-Cross sighed and opened her bag. Ten gold pieces were all she had in the world—but she gave them to Mother Grumpy.

"Where is this Hey-Diddle spell?" she asked. Mother Grumpy went to a cupboard and took down a bottle full of green powder.

"Here it is," she said. "Whoever tastes this will at once start walking to the east, and won't stop until he comes to the palace of the magician Hey-Diddle. Then he will walk into the gates and straightway become the servant of the magician."

"What a powerful spell!" said the old dame, a little frightened. "Where did you get it from?"

"Hey-Diddle gave it to me himself," said Mother Grumpy. "He often wants servants, you know, and he promised me that for every servant he got because of this green powder, he would give me a bag of gold."

"Well, you ought to give it to me for nothing then!" cried Dame Criss-Cross. "You will get heaps of gold because I shall make dozens of children go walking off to his palace to be his servants."

"No, you must pay me," said Mother Grumpy.

"But I will share the bags of gold with you, Dame. That is quite fair. But I want ten gold pieces now to buy a new fly-away broomstick."

Dame Criss-Cross took the Hey-Diddle spell and flew back home on her broomstick. She was very much pleased with her morning's work. Now the next thing to do was to plan how to use the spell.

It was blackberry time just then, and the Dame saw the pixies and elves passing her cottage every day with purple-stained mouths and hands. When she thought of this she clapped her hands in delight.

"I will use the Hey-Diddle spell on a blackberry bush!" she cried. "That's the thing to do! And I'll do it this very night!"

So when it was dark the old woman took her lantern and went to the common. She found a blackberry bush full of ripening berries, and she set her lantern down by it.

"Now first I will make the berries twice as big and black!" she thought, "then the children will be sure to see them and eat them. As soon as I have made the berries big, I will scatter the green powder over the bush and say the words of the Hey-Diddle spell—and when the pixies eat them, their legs will at once march them to the east till they come to Hey-Diddle's palace! Then they will be his servants and nobody will ever know what has become of them! Ha! That will be the end of those nasty, noisy children!"

Dame Criss-Cross danced round the blackberry bush and chanted a magic song. At once all the berries on the bush grew twice as big and became

Dame Criss-Cross shook the bottle of green powder all over the bush, till every blackberry had a speck on it.

very black and juicy. Then the old woman said the words of the Hey-Diddle spell and shook the bottle of green powder all over the bush, till every blackberry had a speck on it.

When the bottle was empty, Dame Criss-Cross put it into her pocket, took up her lantern, and went home very pleased indeed.

The next morning she stood at her window to watch the pixie and elfin children run past. It was a fine day and every single child ran to play on the common.

"Let's pick blackberries, let's pick blackberries!" one cried to another, and the old woman rubbed her hands gleefully.

There were many ripe berries that sunny day and the pixies and elves feasted on them—and suddenly they came to the bush over which Dame Criss-Cross had shaken the Hey-Diddle spell.

"Ooh!" cried a pixie. "Look! Did you ever see such a wonderful crop of blackberries! Why, they are twice as big as any others! Let's pick them and eat them."

"Wait a minute," cried a tall elf, running up. "No, don't let's eat them. My mother has promised to make a pie for the poor old Balloon Man, who is ill—and she asked me to choose the finest I could see. Let's pick them for the old Balloon Man, shall we?"

"Yes, yes!" cried the kind-hearted little creatures. "We won't eat a single one! They shall be made into a wonderful pie for the old Balloon Man!"

So every one of the big blackberries was carefully picked and put into a basket. Then the pixies and elves thought it must be dinner-time, and off they ran to Pinniky Village.

Dame Criss-Cross saw them running past her house, and she was full of surprise and very cross, for she had hoped that not one child would pass that way again—she thought that maybe all of them would be walking eastwards towards Hey-Diddle's palace.

"They can't have found the bush yet," she thought. "I'll just go and see."

So off she went—but when she saw that every berry was gone from it, she stood still in amazement.

"Oh!" she cried. "That wicked Mother Grumpy sold me a spell that was no good! I'll go and see her to-night, and get back my ten gold pieces."

And now what was happening to the blackberries? Why, the tall elf had given them to his mother, and she was already very busy making a pie for the old Balloon Man. When it was finished, she sent the elf to his house.

"Here's a pie for you, Balloon Man!" cried the elf, and handed it in through the window. The Balloon Man was in bed, half asleep. He opened his eyes and nodded, and then fell fast asleep again, without really seeing what the elf had put on the window-ledge. When he woke up, he saw the pie there and was astonished.

"But dear me," he said, "what a pity! The doctor says I mustn't eat pies or tarts this week, so I can't have it. I don't like to send it back to where it came from, for they might be hurt. What shall I do with it?"

He thought for a moment, and then he heard a knock at his door. It was little Tiptap, who was servant to Clippit the bee-woman, just down the road. Tiptap had brought some oranges for the Balloon Man.

"Thank you kindly," said he. "Oh, Tiptap—you might take this pie to Clippit. I mustn't eat pies yet, and it would be a pity to waste it."

So Tiptap ran with the pie to her mistress—but Clippit was quite dismayed to see it.

"Goodness me, Tiptap!" she said, "I've just done all my baking, and I have got four pies cooking in the oven now. I really can't do with another! Whatever shall we do with it?"

"What about Mother Shoo-away and all her children?" asked Tiptap. "I'm sure she would be pleased with it."

"Of course she would!" said Clippit, pleased. "Run along and take it for me, Tiptap."

So Tiptap carried the pie to Mother Shoo-away's cottage. It was almost opposite Dame Criss-Cross's little house, and kind old Mother Shoo-away had often tried to do a good turn to the cross old dame.

"Please," said Tiptap, "here's a pie for you from the bee-woman."

"Oh, thank you!" cried Mother Shoo-away, in delight. "That will be a great treat for my children."

"Ooh!" cried the children, when they saw the big pie. "Ooh! Mother, let's eat it now, shall we?"

"Well, we'll take it out into the garden and eat it

there," said Mother Shoo-away. "It's such a lovely day, and the kitchen is so stuffy."

So out they all trooped into the garden, carrying their plates and spoons. Just as Mother Shoo-away dug her knife into the pie, she caught sight of Dame Criss-Cross standing at her garden gate over the way, and Shoo-away's kind heart made her think that it would be nice to send her a piece of the lovely pie.

"Pinkity," she said to her eldest boy. "Fetch the best plate and the silver spoon from the kitchen. I will send a piece of this pie to poor old Dame Criss-Cross. I'm sure the old woman looks half starved."

Pinkity fetched the best plate and the silver spoon. Mother Shoo-away cut a huge slice of the Hey-Diddle pie and put it on to the plate. The crust was lovely, and the big blackberries made a purple juice over the plate.

"Now run across and give it to Dame Criss-Cross," said Shoo-away to Pinkity. So the pixie went across the road, carrying the plate carefully.

"Please, Dame Criss-Cross," he said politely, "Mother sends you a slice of our pie, and hopes you will like it."

Now Dame Criss-Cross was very hungry, for she had no money left to buy food for herself that day, as she had given it all to Mother Grumpy for the Hey-Diddle spell. So she was glad to see the slice of pie, and for once in a way gave quite a polite message of thanks. Then she started to eat it very hungrily.

Oh, what a good pie it was! What a wonderful

taste it had! Dame Criss-Cross was glad Mother Shoo-away had sent her such a big slice.

Mother Shoo-away was pleased that Dame Criss-Cross had taken the slice of pie. She cut up the rest of the pie, and put it on her children's plates.

"Nobody must begin until you're all served, and we can say grace for such a lovely meal," said Mother Shoo-away to the children. So they all waited patiently. But just as the last child was given his piece of pie, a queer thing happened.

From across the road came a cry of dismay. Mother Shoo-away and the children looked up. They saw Dame Criss-Cross holding on to her gate as hard as she could, whilst her legs seemed to be trying to walk away!

"What's the matter, what's the matter?" cried Mother Shoo-away and the children. They put down their pie and ran to help Dame Criss-Cross.

"It's that horrid pie!" cried the old woman in a rage. "Those Hey-Diddle blackberries have been made into a Hey-Diddle pie—and I've eaten it, I've eaten it! Oh, what shall I do! I'll have to walk to the magician Hey-Diddle's palace now, and be his servant! My legs are taking me! Oh! Oh!"

She had to let go her hold of the gate, and before Mother Shoo-away could stop her the old dame had walked quickly down the lane towards the east, and was soon out of sight.

"Well!" said Mother Shoo-away, who knew perfectly well what a Hey-Diddle spell was, and guessed what mischief the old woman had been up to. "Well! The wicked old dame! She must have bewitched a bush of blackberries, hoping to send all the children who ate them away to the magician Hey-Diddle. But the children must have taken them home for a pie—and somehow it came round to us."

"And we gave a slice to Dame Criss-Cross, and she's the only one who ate it!" cried the children. "So she's been caught by her own spell!"

"What a lucky escape for us!" said Mother Shoo-away. "And oh, how much nicer Pinniky Village will be without Dame Criss-Cross! Let us come and throw away our pie-slices, for we certainly mustn't eat any now."

So the pie was thrown away on the rubbish-heap, and that night an army of rats found it and ate it up, every bit. Then off they went to Hey-Diddle's palace, for the spell was just as strong for them as for anyone else. And how cross the magician was to find rats walking into his bedroom in the middle of the night!

As for Dame Criss-Cross, nobody was ever bothered with *her* again! She had to work from morning to night for the magician, and how he laughed when he heard she had fallen into her own trap! Mother Grumpy was pleased too, because when Hey Diddle sent her a bag of gold, she didn't have to share it with anyone.

And the only person who was miserable was Dame Criss-Cross herself—but she deserved all she got, didn't she?

Chuff the Chimney-Sweep

ONE DAY, right in the middle of the summer, Dick and Janet were walking down the lane that led to the duck-pond. When they came to the big oak tree that stands in the middle of the hedge, they saw a motor car.

But what a strange one! It was very small, smaller even than a baby motor-car, and it was painted bright red, green and yellow. The steering-wheel was yellow, the seats were blue. It really was the gayest little car they had ever seen, and *so* small.

"Why, it's really not much bigger than my toy motor car at home," said Dick. "The one we can both just squeeze into! I wonder who this car belongs to?"

"Let's sit in it for a minute," said Janet. "It

does look so nice. There isn't anyone about, and we'll hop out if we see anyone coming. It would be such fun to pretend it's ours, for a minute or two!"

Now that was naughty of Janet, because she knew perfectly well that she oughtn't to get into other people's cars—but this one looked so lovely and was so bright and gay that she felt she really must.

So Dick got in at the back, and Janet got in at the front, sitting behind the steering-wheel. She took hold of it, pretending to steer—and just at that very moment there came a great noise of shouting behind the hedge, and a gnome came rushing towards them, carrying over his shoulder a pile of poles and brushes.

After him raced a most unpleasant and dirty-looking brownie, whose beard nearly reached the ground. He carried a big stick, and he was shouting very angrily.

"You wait till I catch you, Chuff the chimney-sweep! You wait till I catch you!"

Chuff the gnome tore up to the car, and the astonished children had no time to jump out. The queer little sweep leapt into the car, pushed Janet roughly to one side, took the steering-wheel himself, and started up the engine.

"R-r-r-r-r-r-r!" went the car, and leapt forward down the lane. The angry brownie tripped over his beard just as he reached the car and fell flat on his nose. When he picked himself up the car had gone.

The two children were scared. Whatever was happening? And where were they going? The gnome drove at top speed, and the duck-pond down the lane was passed in a flash. Then up the hill tore the car and down the other side.

"W-w-where are we going?" stammered Janet at last. "You're taking us right away from our lane."

The gnome didn't answer. He looked round to see if the angry brownie was still following, and then made the car go even faster, so that Dick and Janet had to hold on tight, or they would have been shaken out.

"Hie!" shouted Dick, at last, when they had gone quite five miles. "Hie, Chuff the chimney-sweep, stop and let us get out."

Still the gnome took not the slightest notice. He merely hooted loudly at a cow that suddenly walked into the middle of the road. The cow didn't move. The car sped straight towards it. There was no room to pass on either side. The car must either stop or bump into the cow.

Janet and Dick clutched the sides of the car and held their breath. Surely there would be an accident? A car as tiny as Chuff's would break to pieces if it hit a great cow!

Then, to the children's enormous surprise, just as the car was about to hit the cow bang in the middle, Chuff pulled a handle near to Janet, and, hey presto! the car rose high in the air, jumped right over the cow, and landed again with a slight bump on the other side!

"Ooh!" said Dick and Janet, going quite pale. "What a strange car!"

The cow stared at the surprising car and mooed loudly—but in a moment or two it was right away out of sight, and Chuff, Dick and Janet were over the next hill.

The children knew quite well by now that the car was a magic one, and they felt afraid of the strange little chimney-sweep, who drove so fast, jumped over cows, and said never a word. Janet began to wonder however they would get home again, and at last she touched Chuff's arm.

"*Please!*" she said. "*Please!* Do stop for a moment and let us get out."

Chuff waved his hand in front of him.

"Wait till we get to the blue signpost," he said. "Then we shall be safe."

Dick and Janet wondered what he meant. They looked out for the blue signpost, and at last they saw it. Just before they got there something seemed to happen to the car. It slowed down, and began to make a curious grunting noise. The gnome pressed knobs here, and pulled handles there, turning very pale as he did so.

"Get out and push, quick!" he suddenly cried to the two children. "Quick! There's no time to be lost! If our car stops here, that brownie will have us in his power! Push hard to the blue signpost, then we shall be safe!"

Dick and Janet jumped out at once. The car had almost stopped, but not quite. The children ran to the back and began to push. How they pushed! Their faces turned as red as beetroots, because they made themselves so hot. But the car went on moving, and soon it went a little faster.

"Nearly there, nearly there!" cried the gnome. "Go on, go on, we shall be safe in a minute!"

So the children went on pushing, and at last, with a sigh of relief, they found themselves just opposite the blue signpost. The gnome jammed on his brakes and jumped out.

"Phew!" he said, and took out a big yellow handkerchief and mopped his head. "That *was* a near squeak! Another minute and the car would have turned round and gone straight back to that horrid brownie."

"But why?" asked Dick in surprise. "And what made him so angry?"

The gnome laughed till the tears came into his eyes.

"Well, now I'm safe, I don't mind having a good laugh," he said, wiping his eyes. "I'll tell you all about it. I'm Chuff the chimney-sweep, and I go about sweeping chimneys all over the place. Well, Longbeard the brownie wrote and asked me to sweep his, so I went to his cottage this morning. He lives in that big oak tree, you know."

"Oh, *does* he!" said Janet, in surprise. "I didn't know anyone lived there."

"Well, Longbeard does," said Chuff. "I went to him, and I swept two chimneys for him as well as ever I could, and put the soot in a big sack. The chimneys were *terribly* dirty, for they hadn't been swept for years. So I asked Longbeard to pay me sixpence a chimney, which is twice my usual price—but they were really so very dirty, and took me twice as long to do."

"And wouldn't he pay you?" asked Dick.

"No, he wouldn't," said Chuff, frowning. "But I paid him out—ha, ha! ho, ho! I emptied the bag of soot over his head! Ho, ho, ho!"

"So that's why he looked so dirty," said Janet. "Goodness, no wonder he was cross."

"What I didn't remember was that Longbeard owns all the country right up to this blue signpost," said Chuff. "Of course, he wanted to whip me with his stick, but I ran to my car and jumped in—and no sooner was I in it, than I knew that Longbeard would send a spell after me to bring the car back to him—and then he would beat me black and blue, and perhaps turn me into a frog into the bargain."

"So that's why you went so quickly," said Dick.

"Of course," said the gnome. "I had to go faster than the spell, you see. I knew that as soon as I got to the blue signpost, I was safe. But the spell nearly got us. If you hadn't got out and pushed, he would suddenly have swung round and taken us back to Longbeard. Didn't you feel anything of the spell, children, when you were out of the car, pushing it?"

"Yes," said Dick. "I felt as if something was trying to drag my legs backwards."

"Ha, that was it!" said the gnome. "Well, we're safe now. Thank goodness we got away!"

"But how are we going to get back home?" asked Dick. "We are miles away."

"Now I come to think of it, what were you doing in my car?" asked the gnome, looking at them with a frown.

The children went red.

"We thought it was such a dear little car that really we *had* to sit in it for a minute," said Dick. "We didn't know that you were going to come running out in such a hurry."

"Well, I can't possibly take you back yet," said Chuff. "I've got another chimney to sweep at a quarter to twelve, and two more at half-past. What will you do? Will you come with me, and perhaps I can take you home afterwards—or would you rather stay here and try to get a lift back?"

"I think we'd rather come with you," said Janet. "There doesn't seem to be anybody about at all, and if we tried to walk back, I know we should get lost."

"Come on then," said Chuff, getting into the car again. "It's time I was starting off to old Wizard High-in-the-air's!"

They all of them sat in the car again and Chuff started off. For some time they ran along country roads, occasionally passing carriages and cars full of pixies and elves, who started in the greatest astonishment at the two children.

Then suddenly Janet gave a loud cry of surprise, and pointed up in the air.

"Look, Dick, look!" she cried. "There's a castle

on that cloud up there in the sky! Did you ever see such a strange thing?"

Dick looked—and how astonished he was! Far up in the sky was a big purple cloud, and built on it was a stone castle.

"That's where Wizard High-in-the-air lives," said Chuff. "Now look out! Hold tight!"

The little chimney-sweep suddenly pressed the same handle as he had used when jumping over the cow, and to the children's surprise the tiny car rose straight up in the air and went towards the castle on the cloud.

"How does it do it?" asked Dick, when he had got his breath.

"Oh, by magic," said the gnome. "Quite easy when you know how."

It wasn't long before the car reached the cloud, and the gnome turned the handle back again. The car ran on to a narrow road, and went towards the castle. Dick and Janet leaned out to look at the roadway. It was deep purple, and very misty, so that they were puzzled to know how the car could run on it.

"Now you'd better not get out of the car at all," said Chuff, as he stopped before the door of the castle. "You don't know how to walk on this cloudy stuff, and you might fall right through it and find yourselves bump on the ground far below! Be good children and stay here. I don't think the wizard will see you, and I hope he won't. He's not a very pleasant person."

Chuff took his poles and brushes and vanished

into the castle. Presently the children saw a brush come out of one of the chimneys, and they knew that Chuff was hard at work.

Suddenly they heard a voice nearby and saw a curious person looking at them.

"It must be the wizard himself," whispered Janet. "See what a high hat he wears."

"Pray come and drink a cup of milk with me," said the wizard, bowing low.

But Dick and Janet remembered what the gnome had said.

"No, thank you," they said politely. "We are afraid of falling through this purple cloud."

"I will see that you don't," said the wizard. But Dick and Janet wouldn't stir from the car. Then High-in-the-air became angry with them, and began to mutter a string of strange words. To the children's horror, they found that their legs were beginning to move all by themsleves, and against their will they were stepping out of the car!

"Chuff! Chuff! Come quickly!" cried Dick in a panic, fearful of treading on the misty roadway. He held on to the car, whilst one of his legs stepped down to the road. Goodness, it sank deep into the purple road, and Dick knew he would fall right through it.

"Chuff! Chuff!" he called again.

To his great joy he suddenly saw the little chimney-sweep racing down the castle steps, a sack over one shoulder and his brushes over the other.

When he saw what the wizard was doing, he ran straight at him, pushed him over with a brush, and then emptied the soot over his head. Then he leapt into the car, started it up, and drove straight off the cloud down to earth again.

"Well, that's the second person I've emptied soot over to-day," said Chuff. "I shall be making a lot of enemies, there's no doubt of that. So that nasty old wizard was trying to make you go into his castle, was he?"

"Yes," said Dick, "and I was so afraid of falling through the cloud. My leg went right through it."

"So did mine," said Janet. "Oh, I *am* so glad you came when you did, Chuff!"

"Yes, but I've not been paid for the chimney I swept," said the gnome, dolefully. "Never mind. The next place I go to is very nice. It's old Mother Hubbard's. Have you heard of her?"

"Not the one whose cupboard was bare, and she couldn't give her poor dog a bone?" said Dick in surprise.

"The very same," said Chuff. "But she's come into some money since then, you know, and so now her cupboard is always full. She has twenty-four dogs, and feeds them all well. She lives in a little cottage on the top of the hill. It's painted yellow, so look out for it."

They soon saw it, and in about fifteen minutes they pulled up in front of the yellow door. Mother Hubbard came out and welcomed them.

"Why, who are your two friends?" she cried, in surprise, when she saw the children.

"This is Dick, and this is Janet," said Chuff. They all shook hands politely, and Mother Hubbard told the children to sit down on a seat in her little garden.

"You can go and sweep the two chimneys now," said the old woman to Chuff. "And when you've finished, go and wash in the bathroom, and then we'll all sit down to a nice glass of lemonade, and some chocolate buns hot out of the oven!"

Chuff went off to do his work, and the children looked at Mother Hubbard.

"Have you still got that cupboard?" asked Janet.

"Bless you, yes!" said Mother Hubbard, beaming. "Do you mean to say you know about that?"

"Oh, yes," said Dick, and he recited the rhyme about Mother Hubbard and the bare cupboard. She was very much delighted, and took them indoors to see the cupboard. But when she swung the door open, what a sight met their eyes!

The cupboard was full to bursting with good things! There were cakes and puddings, tarts and buns. There were big plates of bones on one shelf, and a tin of biscuits on another.

"Those are for my twenty-four dogs," said Mother Hubbard. "You see, my cupboard isn't bare now, is it?"

"Oh, no," said Dick. "Could we see the dogs, do you think? And have you still got that one who wanted a bone and couldn't have it, because your cupboard was bare?"

"Yes," said the old lady. "Come and see him."

She led them to a yard, and there were the

twenty-four dogs, as bright as new pins, and all wagging their tails like clockwork. The old dame called one dog to her, a little spotted one.

"This is the dear old dog who lived with me when I was so poor," she said. "I love him best of them all."

She let him out of the yard, and he trotted back with them to the garden. By that time, Chuff had finished the chimneys, and they could hear him whistling in the bathroom as he washed himself clean.

"He's nearly ready," said Mother Hubbard. "I'll go and get the lemonade. Stay here for a minute with the dog."

The children played with the dog till Mother Hubbard came back carrying a tray with four glasses of lemonade on it, and a dish of lovely chocolate buns. There was a bone too, and that was for the dog, who at once sat up and begged for it.

Then Chuff came running out, looking very clean, and they all sat down to the lemonade and cakes. How the children did enjoy them—they were quite the nicest buns they had ever tasted, and as for the lemonade, it was delicious.

"Mother Hubbard, what am I to do with these children?" asked Chuff, when they had all finished. "I daren't take them back home in my car, because I'm afraid of meeting Longbeard the brownie again, and I emptied soot over him this morning, so I'm afraid he won't be pleased with me."

"Well, there's a bus running to Blackberry Hill

in a moment or two," said the old lady. "Isn't that near where they live?"

"Yes, that's the hill just behind the duck-pond!" said Dick in surprise. "But I didn't know buses went there! I didn't even know there was a road there! There were only tiny rabbit-paths when Janet and I picked blackberries there last summer."

"Oh, you wouldn't see *our* buses!" said Chuff, laughing. "They are invisible to your eyes when you are out of our land. But hurry up, there's no time to lose. I can hear the bus coming now!"

The children thanked Mother Hubbard and said good-bye. Then they ran off with Chuff to where a small blue bus stood on the hillside. They scrambled on and waved good-bye to the little chimney-sweep.

"R-r-r-r-r!" The bus started off, and soon Mother Hubbard's cottage was lost in the distance. The people in the bus stared at the children, and Dick and Janet stared back too, for the passengers were really very strange.

There was a rabbit, a fox, two pixies, a gnome and three brownies. They all carried baskets, and had been marketing, for their baskets were full. The conductor was a mole, and he gave them two tickets for a penny when they said Blackberry Hill.

It really wasn't very long before they saw that the bus was going up a rabbit-path on Blackberry Hill, and they were astonished to be there so quickly. They jumped out, and were just going to shout good-bye to the other passengers, when to their great amazement they found that the bus had vanished completely, although they could still hear its engine running!

"That's just what the chimney-sweep said," said Janet. "Do you remember, Dick? He said that we couldn't see the pixie buses in *our* land, even though they were there!"

"So he did," said Dick. "Well, come on, Janet, let's race home and tell Mother all we've done this morning."

But Mother really *couldn't* believe them! She said it was all too astonishing.

"Well, Mother, you must come and see Brownie Longbeard in his oak tree," said Janet at last. So they all went next day to the big oak tree in the lane.

But they couldn't find anyone there at all! The tree was hollow, but inside it was quite empty. Janet was *so* disappointed—and then suddenly she spied something on the floor of the tree. It was soot!

"There!" she cried. "That shows you, Mother! Longbeard *was* living here, even if he's gone now! Look at the soot on the floor!"

So Mother had to believe their wonderful story—and the two children are always looking out for Chuff the chimney-sweep, to take him home to tea. But they have never seen him again; isn't it a pity?

The Goblin who Broke his Glasses

Jack and Doris were very sad. It was their mother's birthday the very next day, and they had lost the two shillings and the sixpence that they had saved for seven weeks. They had meant to buy their mother a lovely bottle of scent, and now they could buy her nothing.

"It *is* bad luck!" said Jack. "I had the money in my pocket and I thought it was quite safe there. I didn't know there was a hole at the bottom. The money must have dropped out yesterday when we ran down the grassy hill."

"What are we to do?" asked Doris. "We really *must* buy Mummy something. It would be dreadful if she didn't have a present from us."

"Yes, I know," said Jack. "But I don't see what we can do, Doris. We can't very well ask Mummy for some money to buy her own birthday present with—and Daddy's gone to town."

"Well, we'd better go to the hill we ran down yesterday and try to find the money," said Doris. "That's the only thing *I* can think of!"

So off they went. Very soon they got to the hill, but although they looked simply everywhere they could see no sign of their lost silver at all. They were very disappointed.

"We'd better go home," said Jack, with a sigh. "We'll tell Mummy all about it, then she won't expect a present. We'll tell her that we'll save up again, and give her a lovely bottle of scent as soon as we can. Perhaps she won't mind getting her present later."

So they turned to go back home again. But just as they got half-way down the hill, Doris stopped and clutched Jack's arm.

"Look, Jack!" she said, in a whisper. "What's that over there, sitting on the stile? It isn't a boy and it isn't a man."

Jack looked, and then rubbed his eyes in astonishment. He looked again—but it was quite true; there was a small goblin dressed in green and red, sitting on the stile!

"Why, it's a goblin!" said Jack. "It really is! But Doris, how exciting! We've never seen any of the fairy folk in our lives before, and here is a real, live goblin sitting on a stile!"

The two children stared at the little creature for some time. He didn't move, and he didn't seem to see them. He just sat there quite still.

"Let's go and speak to him," said Doris, feeling very bold. So they walked down the hill to where the stile led into a cornfield. The goblin heard them coming, and he raised his big pointed ears and listened—but still he didn't seem to see them.

"Hullo, Goblin!" said Jack. "I say, are you really a goblin?"

"Of course," said the goblin. "What are you? Children, by the sound of you!"

"Yes, we're children, a girl and a boy," said Jack. "But can't you see us!"

"No," said the goblin, and he blinked his eyes. "I've broken my glasses. I can't see a thing without them. That's why I'm sitting here. I tripped over a stone and fell. My glasses shot off my nose and were smashed to pieces. So I thought if I waited here I should find someone kind enough to lead me safely home. I've another pair of glasses there, you see."

"Well, shall *we* take you home?" asked Doris, kindly. "You could tell us the way to go, couldn't you?"

"Oh, yes," said the goblin, jumping off the stile. "Would you pick up the frame of my glasses, please? Thank you, little girl. I can get some new glass put into them, and then I shall have two pairs again. Now would you each take one of my hands, and lead me carefully home. I will tell you the way."

So they each took one of the goblin's hands and started off.

"Go across the field, and half-way to the next

stile you will see an old oak tree," said the goblin. "Stop just by it, please."

They took him half-way across the field and stopped at the oak tree. The goblin put out his hands and felt all round the trunk. He pressed a knob of bark, and suddenly the whole side of the tree disappeared, and the surprised children saw a stairway inside, leading downwards. They all stepped into the tree, and the trunk closed up again.

There was a lamp hanging above, so Jack and Doris could see their way down. They took the goblin's hands again, and carefully led him downwards.

"When you come to the bottom, you will see three doors," said the goblin. "Open the middle one, and go down the passage beyond. You will soon come to some toadstools. Choose three red ones side by side, and we will sit upon them."

It was just as the goblin said. At the end of the stairway were three doors, one painted yellow, one red and one green. The middle one was yellow, and the children opened it. Beyond was a narrow, winding passage. They all went down it, and came to a large cave in which toadstools of every colour grew. They were very large and Jack looked all about for three red ones side by side. He found them at last, and led the goblin towards them.

The three sat down on the toadstools, and the goblin muttered some magic words. Suddenly they all shot upwards at a terrific pace, and Jack and Doris gasped for breath. Up and up went the toadstools, and then came to a stop out in the open air.

"Here we are," said the gnome. "Now, if you'll kindly take my hands again, and lead me to the fifth cottage in the row by the beech tree, that's the end of our journey."

Jack and Doris saw a higgledy-piggledy row of funny little cottages in the shade of a large beech tree. They led the goblin to the fifth one, which was called Ho-ho Cottage, and the little man took out a key. He unlocked the front door, and went inside. When he came out he was wearing a very large pair of round glasses.

"That's better!" he said. "Now I can see properly! It's dreadful not to be able to see anything. Will you please come in and have some chocolate cake and a glass of lemonade?"

The children were delighted. They went inside Ho-ho Cottage and sat down. It was the tiniest little place. The goblin brought out a very large chocolate cake and a jug of lemonade. Jack and Doris were soon munching hungrily.

"Wasn't it lucky for you we were on the hill?" said Doris. "You might have waited all day before anyone passed, because very few people go that way."

"What were you doing there?" asked the goblin. Jack told him all about the lost two shillings and sixpence, and how sorry they were not to be able to buy anything for their mother's birthday.

"Dear, dear, that's very sad," said the goblin. "But wait now! I have an idea! I could show you

The goblin brought out a very large chocolate cake and a jug of lemonade.

where some very fine mushrooms grow. You could pick them, and then sell them at the market, couldn't you? The money you get for them would buy your mother a fine present! Would you like that?"

"Ooh, yes!" said both the children together.

So when they had finished their cake and lemonade, the goblin took them outside.

"Wait a minute!" he said. "You haven't a basket with you. I'll lend you my biggest one, but would you mind letting me have it back? You could leave it outside that old oak-tree in the field for me."

"Yes, we will," said Jack. The goblin fetched a fine big basket, and they all set off together. They went back the way they had come, and when they had reached the cornfield, the goblin took them to a green meadow not very far away. And there, near to a ditch, was the finest crop of mushrooms the children had ever seen.

"I'll leave you now if you don't mind," said the goblin. "I've got to go and see my tailor about a new coat. Good luck to you, and mind you pick all the mushrooms you want! Thank you for being kind to me."

"Good-bye, and thank you too!" cried the children. "Don't forget to get your glasses mended!"

The goblin vanished. The two children set to work to pick the mushrooms. It was not long before they had a big basket full to the brim.

"Now we'll go to the market," said Jack. "We'll

carry the basket between us. Isn't it heavy, Doris!"

When they got to the market, they went to a farmer's wife they knew, who had a stall with greens, butter and jars of cream spread out on it. She cried out in surprise when she saw the mushrooms.

"Lawkamussy me, where *did* you get those wonderful mushrooms?" she cried. "You sell them to me before anyone else sees them! I'll give you a good price for them!"

The children were glad to empty the basket into her box. She weighed the mushrooms, and then said she would give them three shillings for the lot.

"Oh, that's lovely!" cried Jack. "Sixpence more than we had before! Oh, thank you, Mrs. Mooly."

The farmer's wife paid them, and they ran off to the shop that sold perfume. They bought a lovely bottle of lavender water for their three shillings, and then turned to go home, for it was getting near their dinner-time. They took the goblin's basket with them, and when they came to the oak tree they left it outside as the goblin had asked them.

Their mother was so pleased with her birthday present next day.

"My favourite perfume!" she cried. "Oh, you kind children! But, my dears, how did you manage to buy it? Daddy told me you had lost your money."

Then the children told her about the little goblin, and she could hardly believe her ears.

"We'll go this very morning to that old oak tree and try to find the stairway inside!" she said.

So off they went. The basket was gone, of course,

for the goblin had fetched it the night before. The children tried hard to find the knob of bark that would make the side of the tree disappear, but they couldn't. Wasn't it a pity?

"We'll find it *one* day!" cried Jack. "And then hurrah for another exciting adventure!"

Heyho and the North Wind

ONCE upon a time Heyho the brownie was washing his clothes on a very windy day. He washed a pair of blue socks, six blue handkerchiefs, a red shirt and a yellow tunic. Then he took up his lovely new scarf, and put that into the soapy water too.

Heyho was very proud of his scarf. It was yellow with an orange border, and was the nicest one in the whole of his village. The Fairy Queen herself had given it to him for a present when he had once stopped her runaway rabbits. They were pulling her carriage, and had been frightened at something —and off they went through the woods, helter-skelter, with the frightened Queen pulling hard at the reins.

Then Heyho had run out from the bushes and

caught hold of the reins, stopping the rabbits at once. The Queen was very grateful, and by the next post had come the lovely yellow scarf in return for the brownie's bravery.

So you can guess Heyho was proud of it, and he washed it very carefully indeed. Then he wrung it out, and hung it up on the line to dry. Eight-legs the Spider had lent him his strongest thread, and it made a very nice washing line.

Heyho emptied his wash-tub and put the soap away. Then he went indoors to make himself a cup of cocoa, for he was rather thirsty after so much washing.

"It's a good thing it's such a windy day," said Heyho to himself. "It will dry the clothes quickly."

"Whoo-oo-oo!" roared the wind outside. It was the North Wind, and it sounded excited. It flapped the clothes to and fro and they all danced up and down.

Heyho finished his cocoa and went outside to see if his clothes were drying. He felt the socks—yes, nearly dry. He felt the handkerchiefs—yes, *quite* dry—and the tunic and shirt were hardly wet at all—and the scarf—but dear me, *where* was the scarf?

Heyho's heart almost stopped beating. He looked up and down the line, but there was no scarf to be seen. It was gone! What a dreadful thing!

The pegs were still there. The North Wind must have torn the scarf away and taken it for himself!

"He saw it and thought it would do for him nicely, I expect," thought Heyho. "Oh my lovely,

lovely scarf that the Queen gave me! I *must* get it back, I really must!"

He sat down on the grass and wondered how he could get it back. He scratched his chin hard, rubbed his nose, and frowned deeply. Then he had an idea.

"I'll go to the North Wind's house and ask him what he has done with it!" he said, jumping to his feet. "He has no right to steal my scarf like that! I'll make him give it back to me!"

So he locked up his little house, and took the key to Twiddle, his next-door neighbour.

"Where are you going, all of a sudden?" asked Twiddle in surprise.

"To the house of the North Wind," said Heyho, fiercely. "He has stolen my scarf, and I'm going to get it back!"

"Oh, Heyho, you *are* brave!" cried Twiddle. "The North Wind is very big and very strong. I should be afraid to go and see him. People say that he has a dreadful temper, too!"

"Well, I hope I come back all right," said Heyho, feeling a bit shaky. "Anyway, here's my key, Twiddle. Keep it for me, will you?"

So Twiddle said he would, and Heyho marched off northwards. He went up seven hills and down again. He crossed ten rivers and went over twelve stiles. He walked through five woods and then far away in the distance he saw the mountain on the top of which was the house of the North Wind.

It was very cold. Snowflakes floated about in the air, and Heyho wished that he had his nice warm scarf tied tightly round his neck. He felt very cross indeed with the North Wind. He began to climb the mountain, and soon he was quite out of breath. He would never have got to the top if a large eagle had not kindly offered him a lift.

"My nest is nearly at the top," said the eagle. "I will take you as far as that, if you like."

So Heyho gladly climbed on to the bird's soft back, and soon he was nearly at the top of the steep mountain. The eagle shook him off, and he said thank you, and went on again up the winding path.

Soon he saw the house of the North Wind. It was a funny sort of house, for, although it had openings for windows and doors, it had no glass in the windows and no doors in the entrances. Heyho thought it must be a very cold house to live in.

At last he got to the front doorway. He could see no sign of the North Wind, but he heard a loud snoring noise. He peeped in at the front doorway, and at first saw nothing. Then made out a great bed, and lying on it was the North Wind, an enormous person, very billowy looking. He was fast asleep and snoring.

"Oh dear!" thought Heyho. "He won't be very pleased at being wakened up."

The brownie stood and looked at the North Wind for a few minutes, and then he made up his mind. He *must* wake him! So he stepped into the doorway and went up to the bed.

"Hie, North Wind!" he said. "Wake up!"

The North Wind didn't stir. So Heyho shouted more loudly still:

"HIE, NORTH WIND! WAKE UP, I SAY!"

He poked the North Wind with his finger and made him stir. Then with an enormous yawn the Wind sat up and rubbed his eyes. He looked so big that Heyho's knees began to shake, and he could hardly stand up.

Then the North Wind suddenly saw Heyho, and stared in surprise.

"What did you wake me for?" he asked, crossly.

"I've come to ask you to give me back my yellow scarf," said Heyho, boldly. "You took it this morning."

"What! You've come to wake me up for a silly thing like that!" cried the North Wind, angrily. "I'll blow you to the other end of the world!"

He stooped down and was just going to blow the brownie right out of the house, when Heyho caught hold of his nose and held on tight. That just saved him, for though he was lifted right off his feet by the force of the wind, he wasn't blown away.

"Ow! Oh!" cried the North Wind. "Let go my nose, you horrid little brownie!"

"Well, don't blow me away, then!" said Heyho. "And let me tell you this, North Wind—the Fairy Queen will be very angry when she hears that you have taken my scarf. She gave it to me herself!"

"Ooh!" said the North Wind. "I didn't know that. The Fairy Queen, did you say? Well, well! Why didn't you tell me that at first?"

"You didn't give me a chance," said the brownie.

"You nearly blew me to the end of the world!"

"Well, I'm very sorry about your scarf," said the North Wind. "As a matter of fact, I *did* take it! It looked so gay hanging there that I thought I'd like a game with it. So I pulled it off the line and blew it right away."

"Oh dear!" said Heyho. "Do you know where it is now!"

"Well, I left it hanging over Wizard Wimple's chimney," said the North Wind. "It looked very funny there, I can tell you."

"My poor scarf!" groaned Heyho. "Well, you'll have to take me to Wizard Wimple's to get it back, North Wind."

"Easy!" cried the Wind, and lifted Heyho up into the air in a trice. He blew him along at a terrific speed and put him down bump, just outside Wizard Wimple's cottage. Heyho looked up at the chimney—but alas! There was no yellow scarf there!

"That's funny!" said the North Wind. "Let's go and ask what he's done with it."

"*You* go!" said Heyho, nervously. "I'm not very fond of wizards."

So the North Wind banged at the door, and the Wizard's black cat answered it.

"Where's that scarf that was hanging over the chimney?" demanded the North Wind.

"So it was *you* who put it there!" said the cat. "Well, my master was very cross about it. He has given it to Witch Deep-eyes to make a spell with. She wanted a scarf just like that."

"Oh dear!" cried Heyho in dismay. "Quick, North Wind, take me to Witch Deep-eyes before she uses my lovely scarf for her horrid spells."

The North Wind caught up Heyho once more and blew him off to Witch Deep-eyes' cottage in the middle of a thick wood. He knocked at the door, and the witch looked out of the window.

"What do you want ?" she asked crossly.

"The yellow scarf that the Wizard gave you," answered the Wind. "Have you used it for a spell yet?"

"No," said the witch. "It wasn't quite the right colour after all. So I gave it to Mr. Biscuits, the man who sells me my bread. He lives at the other side of the wood."

She banged the window down, and the Wind turned to poor Heyho.

"Well, we'd better go to Mr. Biscuits," he said. "My, this is a journey, isn't it!"

Off they went again, and soon arrived at Mr. Biscuits'. He was baking bread in his shop, and when he came out to see them he was covered with flour.

"Do you want to buy my loaves?" he asked.

"No," said the Wind. "We want that yellow scarf that Witch Deep-eyes gave you. It belongs to Heyho."

"Oh, I gave it to my little girl, Cherry Bun," said Mr. Biscuits. "She has gone on an errand to Mother Buttercup, up on the hill."

"We'll go and meet her," said the Wind. So once again Heyho was whisked off. He was put down just by a little girl—but she was not wearing the yellow scarf.

"Is your name Cherry Bun?" asked the North Wind. "Well, where's that yellow scarf, little girl?"

"I've g-g-given it to my f-f-friend," said Cherry Bun, rather frightened to see such an enormous person as the North Wind. "The colour didn't suit me, and she gave me a little blue purse in exchange. Would you like that instead?"

She held out the purse, but Heyho shook his head.

"No, I want my scarf," he said. "Where does your friend live?"

"In Higgledy Village over there," said Cherry Bun. So off went the Wind and the brownie once more. They soon arrived at Higgledy, and asked for Cherry Bun's friend. When they found her, they looked in vain for the scarf.

"Oh, an elf came by and saw me wearing it and he said it didn't belong to me, so he took it away," said the little girl, with tears in her eyes. "I don't know where he went to."

"I'm hungry and tired," said the North Wind. "Let's buy some buns and chocolate, Heyho, and have a picnic."

So they did, and after that they felt better. Then they hunted all over the countryside for the elf, but couldn't find him.

"Well, I'm really very sorry," said the North Wind. "But I don't see that I can do any more for you, Heyho, except take you home. I'm very tired, and I want to go back and finish my sleep."

So he took Heyho home, and set him down on his own front doorstep—and oh dear me, whatever do you think! Why, tied tightly round Heyho's bright knocker was his lovely yellow scarf! Someone had put it there for him!

"*Well!*" cried the North Wind, crossly. "Here it is after all! And you needn't have wakened me up, and made me rush round the country like that, after all! I've a good mind to blow you to the end of——"

"Oh, no, you won't," said Heyho. "It was your fault to begin with, North Wind! You just go right back and finish your sleep, and don't be so cross!"

The North Wind puffed Heyho's hat off and then flew away to his house on the mountin. Heyho picked up his hat, untied his scarf, and went to Twiddle's house to get his key.

"Oh!" said Twiddle when he opened the door. "I'm so glad you're back, Heyho—and you needn't have bothered about your scarf after all! I happened to be walking out to-day, and I saw a little girl wearing your lovely scarf. So I made her give it to me and brought it back for you—and I expect you found it tied round your door knocker, didn't you?"

"Yes, I did," said Heyho. "Thank you, Twiddle."

He took his key, unlocked his little front door, and made himself a cup of cocoa.

"*Well!*" he said. "To think I've had all that flying about for nothing! I might just as well have stayed at home and read my new story-book!"

And so he might!

Pippy and the Gnome

ONE DAY, when Billy and Joan were playing at Red Indians in the garden, and were wearing bands of feathers round their heads, a very funny thing happened.

Billy was crawling along in the grass, pretending to follow an enemy, and Joan was just behind him. All at once they heard a tiny shout, and running through the grass at top speed came a little pixie in green. At first he didn't see Billy and Joan, for he kept looking behind him in terror. Something was chasing him!

He bumped right into Billy, and gave a scream of fright.

"Don't be afraid," said the little boy. "I won't hurt you. What's the matter?"

"Oh, please, that horrid gnome is after me

again," panted the little pixie. "Could you hide me, please? I haven't done anything wrong, really I haven't! Oh, do save me!"

"I'll slip you into my pocket!" said Joan. "You're just small enough!"

So she picked up the frightened pixie and in a trice he had disappeared into her pocket, where he lay as still as a mouse.

No sooner was he there than the grass was parted in front of Billy, and a most unpleasant-looking gnome peeped through. He seemed surprised to see the little boy, and made a very ugly face at him. Billy frowned.

"What do you want in our garden?" he said, sternly. "And don't you know that it is very rude to make faces?"

The gnome went red with anger, and made a curious snorting noise.

"What do you mean, *your* garden!" he said. "It's *my* garden, I'd like you to know. Haven't I had a house here for the last two hundred years? *Your* garden indeed! And let me tell you this, little boy. I shall make as many faces as I like, so there!"

He made another ugly face, and Billy laughed.

"You're very silly," he said. "And I'm not a bit frightened of you. I only wish that a nice fairy or pixie lived here instead of you."

"Have you seen a pixie anywhere about?" asked the gnome.

"I shouldn't tell you if I had," answered Billy.

"Nor should I," said Joan.

"Well, if you've hidden him, I'll punish you!" said the nasty little gnome, shaking his fist. "He's a very bad pixie indeed. He's a robber, that's what he is! He stole one of my very best spells once, and if ever I get hold of him I'll turn him into an earwig!"

"Well, I don't wonder he's afraid of you," said Joan. "If I was as little as he is, I'd run away too!"

"How do you know he is little?" cried the gnome sharply. "Ha! You've seen him then! You're hiding him! You naughty girl, give him to me at once!"

He rushed at Joan, and she cried out in fright. At once Billy fitted an arrow to his Red Indian bow and pointed it at the angry gnome.

"Come any nearer and I'll shoot!" he said. "Leave my little sister alone. Go away at once and never come back, or I'll tell my Daddy and he'll set a mouse-trap for you!"

The gnome was frightened when he saw Billy's bow and arrow. He turned and ran off at once, shouting all the time. Billy was very glad to see him go.

"Quick!" he said to Joan. "Let's take the pixie to the summer-house before that gnome comes back."

They ran to the summer-house, and Joan took the pixie from her pocket. He was very grateful to them, and thanked them over and over again.

"I'm not a robber," he said. "The gnome is very wicked and powerful, and he made a strong spell that could turn every fairy into an ant or a wasp. I got to hear of it, so I crept in at his window one night, on the orders of the Fairy Queen, and took it away to destroy it. It would never do for the lovely fairies to be nothing but insects, would it?"

"Of course not!" said Billy. "But, little pixie, why don't you go away from this place, for the gnome means to catch you, you know."

"I shall soon," said the pixie. "But I have a friend here, a sandy rabbit, and as he has been ill, I have been looking after him. He is better now, so I shall be going away in a few days' time. I will come and say good-bye to you on Thursday morning at ten o'clock, under the laburnum tree. Will you be there?"

"Of course we will," said Joan and Billy together. Then the pixie ran off and disappeared. The children looked at one another.

"*Well!*" said Billy. "Who would have thought of having such an adventure as that! Nobody would believe us if we told them!"

"Then don't let's tell them!" said Joan.

So they decided not to say a word to anyone, and they waited excitedly for Thursday morning to come, for they both wanted to ask the pixie many questions about Fairyland and the Fairy Queen.

When Thursday morning came at last they ran to the laburnum tree, and waited there at half-past nine, for they wanted to be sure of being in time. After a while they heard the church clock chime out the hour, and then they listened whilst it struck ten.

They looked round for the pixie, but they couldn't see him.

Five minutes went by, and still he didn't come.

"Perhaps he's still saying good-bye to his friend the sandy rabbit," said Billy.

"Or perhaps he's forgotten to come!" said Joan.

"Oh, no!" Billy said. "I'm sure he wouldn't do that. Let's wait a bit longer."

So they waited for ten minutes and then for fifteen, and still the little pixie didn't come. Then they began to feel rather worried about him.

"I do hope that horrid gnome hasn't got him after all!" said Billy.

"Oh, dear! That's just what I was——" began Joan, and then she stopped in astonishment, and pointed down the garden. Billy looked to see what she was pointing at—and what *do* you think he saw? Why, a big sandy rabbit, holding a blue handkerchief to his streaming eyes, sobbing very loudly indeed, as he came slowly towards the children.

"Oh, what's the matter?" cried Billy, running to meet him. "Has anything happened to the pixie?"

The rabbit wiped his eyes, and answered in a sobbing voice.

"Y-y-yes, little boy. The Google Gnome has g-g-got him. Oh, boo-hoo-hoo! I thought I'd come and tell you, and see if you c-c-could help him."

"Don't cry so," said Joan, gently. "We'll help you if we can. Tell us what happened."

"Well," began the rabbit, wiping his eyes again, "well—oh, boo-hoo-hoo!"

He began to cry again, and the two children thought he would never stop.

"Have my handkerchief," said Joan. "Yours is so wet that it can't possibly hold any more tears. And do try to stop crying, rabbit dear, because if you don't, we can't help the pixie."

"N-n-no!" said the rabbit, taking Joan's handkerchief and giving her his. "Well, I'll t-t-tell you. You see, the pixie was—oh, boo-hoo-hoo!"

"We shall never know what has happened!" said Billy, impatiently. "Quick, rabbit, tell us and don't be a cry-baby."

At last the rabbit managed to tell them what had happened.

"My friend, Pippy the pixie, was just saying good-bye to me this morning," he said, "and was telling me that he was going to see you at ten o'clock under the laburnum when my door-bell rang. Pippy went to see who was at the door, and there was that horrid Google with a big green sack. He popped Pippy into it and ran off with him. I ran after them for a long way, but the gnome was too clever for me. He just disappeared! Then I came to ask you to help me."

"I *thought* that old gnome would get Pippy," said Billy. "Now, what can we do, rabbit?"

"My name's Whiskers," said the rabbit, giving Joan her handkerchief back, and tying his own wet one round his neck like a muffler.

"Well, what can we do, Whiskers?" asked Billy. "I don't see how we can rescue Pippy, because we don't know where he has gone."

"We can soon find out," said Whiskers, looking more cheerful. "I will take you to where I last saw Google, and then we'll ask if anyone saw him going on his way. You'd better make yourselves small though, or else you'll never be able to walk down the fairy paths."

"But how can we do that?" asked Billy, in surprise.

"Easy!" said the rabbit. He joined their hands together, told them three magic words to say with their eyes shut, and then placed a clover leaf on their heads.

Billy said the three magic words and so did Joan. Then, hey presto! They suddenly felt as if they were going down in a lift, and when they opened their eyes, they found that they had grown very small indeed, even smaller than Whiskers the rabbit, who was standing just by them, smiling for the first time. They were still in their garden, but how different it seemed! The grass was up to their shoulders, and the trees seemed to touch the sky!

"How queer!" said Joan, in excitement. "Oh, what an adventure we're having, Billy!"

"Yes," said Billy. "But we must be careful not to get caught by Google the gnome ourselves, Joan. He's not very fond of us, you know!"

"Come on," said Whiskers, and he led the way down the garden. He disappeared down a hole in a bank, and the children followed. It was the rabbit's burrow, and very dark indeed.

"Hold on to my bobtail," said Whiskers. So they held on fast and at last arrived at his house underground. They did not stop there, but at once took the way that Google the gnome had gone with Pippy. Up another hole they went and came out into a wood. The bluebells were all out, and stood higher than Billy and Joan. They made a tiny tinkling noise very pleasant to hear.

"This is where I lost sight of them," said Whiskers at last, and he stopped under a bramble bush. "Now let's see if anyone is about that we can ask for help."

"Are you looking for the Google Gnome?" suddenly cried a voice above them. The children and Whiskers looked up and saw an elf hanging out clothes to dry on a line of bramble a good way overhead. "I saw the way he went. He went to Hollow Tree Station, and I expect he caught a train there!"

"Oh, thank you!" cried Whiskers, and hurried the children onwards till he came to a very big tree. It was hollow inside, and the rabbit opened a tiny door, and pushed the children inside. They went down a long winding staircase, and then, to their immense surprise, found themselves in a small station underground.

Whiskers went up to a porter, who had two lovely silver wings growing out of his uniform, and asked him if the Google Gnome had caught a train there just lately.

"Yes," said the porter. "He took the train to Gloomy Castle. He had a large sack with him, which he said was full of new potatoes."

"Oh, the story-teller!" said the rabbit, shocked.

"Well, thank goodness we know where he's gone. When's the next train for Gloomy Castle, please?"

"It's just coming in now," said the little porter, and sure enough a train clanked in at that minute. All the carriages were without roofs, and the children quickly scrambled into one near the engine, looking surprised at the passengers in the carriages. There were fairies and elves, many rabbits, two or three moles, a hedgehog with a whole carriage to himself, and four people who looked like witches and carried large broomsticks.

Off went the train, and after three stations it arrived at Gloomy Castle. The children got out, and the rabbit took them up a little stairway, into the open air. And there, perched on a nearby hill, was the Gloomy Castle!

It was built of black stones, and a cloud hung over the top of it, for it was very tall. A steep path led up to it, and Whiskers led the way towards it.

"This castle belongs to Google," he said. "It has no doors and no windows, so that unless Google himself by a spell makes a door appear, no one can enter it."

"But how in the world are we to rescue Pippy, then?" asked Joan, puzzled.

"Ha!" said the rabbit, in a pleased voice. "I've been thinking that out in the train. You wait till we reach the castle!"

They climbed up the steep path, and at last came to the black walls. Not a door or window was to be seen. Billy turned to the rabbit.

"Well, *I* don't see how we can get in," he said.

"Listen, then," said Whiskers. "I'm a rabbit aren't I? And rabbits can burrow, can't they? Well, what about digging a hole right under the walls, and getting in that way? Isn't that a clever idea?"

"Yes!" said both the children, and they patted the rabbit on the back. "That's a splendid idea! Hurry up and begin."

In a trice the rabbit began digging at the foot of the wall, sending out showers of earth with his hind feet. The children watched him in delight. Down he went and down, and then at last he called out to them.

"I've come to the end of the wall's foundations!" he said. "Now I'm going underneath. Be ready to follow, won't you? I expect we shall arrive in the cellar."

It didn't take long for Whiskers to make a tunnel into the cellar, and the two children climbed into the hole and followed him. They found themselves in a dark, damp place, and for the first time they felt a little frightened.

"There are some steps here," whispered the rabbit. "Come on! Up we go!"

They slowly went up the steps, and came to a door at the top. The rabbit swung it open and peered out into a brightly lighted hall. There were doors all round, and in the middle was a spiral staircase going up to the next floor.

There was no one about, so the three stepped quietly into the hall, their hearts beating very fast indeed. Just as they were wondering what to do next, they heard voices, and footsteps sounded on the spiral stairway.

"It's Google himself!" said Whiskers in a panic. "Quick, we must hide!"

He opened the door nearest to him, and the two children squeezed in behind him. They found themselves in a cupboard in which hung coats and cloaks and hats. They hid themselves behind the biggest cloaks, and waited there, trembling.

Google was talking to someone. He came right down the stairs and stood in the hall. The children heard everything he said.

"Well, you shall have the spells you want by to-morrow morning, Wizard," he said. "Good-bye! Oh, wait a minute! Have you seen my new cloak of invisibility? Whoever wears it can't be seen, you know. I'll just show it to you!"

To the children's horror he opened the door of their cupboard and came in! They hardly dared to breathe. The gnome looked all round the coats and cloaks, and almost trod on Billy's foot when he took down a big blue cloak. He went out and showed it to the wizard, who admired it very much. Then Google made a door appear in the wall of his castle, and the wizard went out, calling good-bye.

The gnome opened the cupboard door again, and threw the cloak on to a peg. Then he slammed the door, and went away. How glad the children and the rabbit were! They had been very much frightened.

"I say!" said Whiskers, at last. "Wasn't that a narrow squeak? I'm shaking all over!"

"So am I!" said Billy. "But I've got an idea! Let's throw this magic cloak round us, so that we can't be seen, and go and see if we can find out where Pippy is!"

"Ooh, yes!" said Joan and Whiskers together. So they quickly threw the cloak around them, opened the door and stole out. Google was nowhere to be seen.

The three tried every door in the hall and opened each one. But the rooms were empty. Then they went up the stairs, and tried the doors there. All empty. They tried on the next floor and the next and not a single sign did they see of Google or Pippy. The only live thing they found was a large black cat sitting by a fire in one room. It hissed in fright when it saw the door opening by itself and no one there.

At last, rather tired, the children and Whiskers reached the topmost floor of all. Here there was only one door. Voices came from behind it, and Whiskers pricked up his ears.

"Pippy's there, and so is Google," he whispered "Oh, I hope we rescue him in time!"

At that moment the door opened, and out came Google. He could not see the children or the rabbit, for the magic cloak was round them. He locked the door, and was just about to put the key in his pocket when Billy put out his hand and grabbed it.

Google was startled, and nearly jumped out of his skin! He could see no one, and his key had vanished into the air, for Billy had quickly put it into his own pocket. The gnome gave a howl of fright, and tore down the stairs.

"Oh, good!" said Whiskers. "Now we can unlock the door and rescue Pippy! He can get under the cloak with us and we can all escape unseen!"

Billy slipped the key into the lock, opened the door and looked into the room. The others followed him in. They stared round the big room, but, to their great surprise, they could see no one at all!

"That's strange!" said Joan. "There was someone talking to Google when he was here, wasn't there, Whiskers?"

"Yes!" said the rabbit. "It was Pippy, I know. But where can he be?"

And then at that moment they saw—what do you think! A little brown earwig on the floor, hurrying towards them! They all looked at it—and then Whiskers burst into tears.

"It's poor Pippy!" he sobbed. "Oh, look, the horrid gnome has changed him into an earwig. Oh dear, oh dear! Now what are we to do?"

They were all shocked and sorry. It was dreadful.

"Stay here!" said Billy, suddenly. "I'll take the cloak and go down to that wicked gnome! I'll just see if I can't put things right!"

He flung the magic cloak round his shoulders, and ran down the stairs, leaving the others staring after him. Down and down he went till he came to the hall. One of the doors was open, and he peeped in. The gnome was bending over a large book, reading it. Billy crept into the room and suddenly banged the door. Google looked up in surprise. He thought that there must be someone outside the door, so he ran to see. In a trice Billy slammed the door again, and locked it on the inside, so that the gnome could not get into the room—for Billy had seen that the book the gnome was reading was a book of magic!

"I'll just find out how to change poor Pippy back to his own shape!" he thought. He saw that Google had been looking up "Disappearing Keys and How to Get Them Back," and he smiled to think that the gnome had no idea where his key had gone. Quickly he turned up the page marked "EARWIGS," and read what to do to change people back to their own shape.

The gnome was outside all this time, hammering at the door. Billy was just going to open it, when he suddenly thought of something else. He quickly looked into the magic book again, and found "Wicked Gnomes and How to Punish Them." He copied out a magic word on a bit of paper, slipped it into his pocket, and then ran to the door. He opened it, and the gnome rushed inside, furious with rage, looking all round for Billy.

But of course he couldn't see him, because of the magic cloak. The little boy slipped out of the room, and ran upstairs again to the top of the castle, where the others were anxiously awaiting him.

Soon he had spoken the seven magic words that changed earwigs to pixies, and hey presto! the earwig vanished, and before them stood Pippy the pixie, tears streaming down his cheeks at the sight of his brave rescuers.

"Quick, there's no time to be lost!" said Billy, wrapping the big blue cloak round all four of them. "We must escape before the gnome thinks of some spell to stop us. Hurry now!"

Down they all went, and when they got to the hall they could hear the gnome stamping round his room still looking for the person who had locked him out of it. He didn't guess that Billy had worn the magic cloak!

The two children, the pixie and the rabbit hurried down the cellar steps, and the rabbit led the way to the tunnel he had made under the wall. In a few moments they were all safely out in the sunshine.

"Now watch!" said Billy, taking the piece of paper that had the magic word written on it, from his pocket. "This is a spell that punishes wicked gnomes!"

He said the long word carefully—and then lo and behold! The great black castle exploded with a tremendous bang, flew into the air, and vanished in smoke. Where the wicked gnome went to nobody knew, but it is certain he was never seen again.

Then back they all went by train to the hollow tree, and walked through the wood home again. Pippy could not thank Billy and Joan enough for coming to his rescue, and as for the rabbit, he wouldn't stop talking he was so excited!

"You shall both come to the very next party that the Fairy Queen gives!" said Pippy, as he said good-bye to the children. "Thank you *very* much for your kindness! I'll come and fetch you on the night of the party, so look out for me on a moonlight night."

And you can think of Billy and Joan enjoying themselves in Fairyland the next time that the moon is full. Won't they have fun!

The Enchanted Bellows

ONCE upon a time there were two little imps called Bubble and Squeak. They lived in Puff Cottage, and they made bellows. They sold them for a penny each, and made quite a lot of money. They carved animals on the handles, and all the fairies came to buy them because they were so well made and pretty.

Now Bubble was good and Squeak was naughty. Squeak was always trying to make Bubble do things he shouldn't, but usually Bubble wouldn't do them. Then one day Squeak had a very strange idea.

"Bubble!" he said, in an excited whisper. "Let's get a wind spell from the Blowaway Witch, and put it into a pair of bellows! Then we'll sell them to someone we don't like, and see what happens!"

"Don't be naughty," said Bubble. "And stop whispering in my ear like that. It tickles."

"But Bubble, oh Bubble, do let's!" said Squeak. "It's the loveliest idea I've ever had. Just think how funny it would be to put a spell into a pair of bellows! Why, they'd blow and blow and blow all by themselves, and it would be such a joke."

Squeak began to laugh, and when he laughed Bubble simply had to do the same, because Squeak's laugh went on and on like a bubbling stream. And as soon as Bubble began to laugh he felt as naughty as Squeak.

"All right," he said, when he had got his breath again. "Let's go to the Blowaway Witch now, before I change my mind."

So off they went. The Blowaway Witch lived on the top of a steep hill, and was friends with the South Wind. There was always a breeze round her cottage and her chimney smoke never went straight up into the sky. It was always blown this way and that.

The two imps were very much out of breath when they at last reached the cottage. They knocked at the door, and the witch came to open it.

"What do you want?" she said.

"Please could you let us have a wind-spell?" asked Squeak.

"What for?" asked the Witch.

"To put into one of our pairs of bellows," said Bubble, going red.

"But that would be naughty," said the witch. "Besides, the spell is sixpence, and I am sure you haven't so much money as that."

"Yes, we have," said Squeak, and he took out a bright new sixpence. "Please let us have the spell, dear witch."

Just at that moment the South Wind came to the door too, for he happened to be having tea with the Blowaway Witch, and had heard all that the imps had said.

"Give them the spell," he said. "They can't do any harm with it!"

So the witch took down her box of spells, and looked inside for a wind-spell. She took out one that was not very strong, but just as she was going to hand it to Bubble, she dropped it. The South Wing picked it up, but before he gave it to the imps he breathed on it.

"That will make it ten times as strong as the strongest wind-spell that ever was made!" he thought to himself in glee, for he was a very mischievous fellow. "They will get more than they bargain for! What fun!"

The two imps knew nothing of this. They took the spell, said thank you, paid the witch, and went off down the hill. When they got home they made a fine pair of bellows with ducks carved on the handles, and then with much laughter they pushed the wind-spell right into the very middle of the bellows.

"Now as soon as anyone uses these, the wind-spell will start working, and blow everything all about the room!" chuckled Bubble and Squeak. "Ooh, wouldn't we like to see it!"

They wondered who would buy the bellows, and they decided to wait until someone they didn't like at all came along. And that someone arrived the very next day.

It was Grunts, the old gnome from the bluebell wood. He was very bad-tempered and rude, and the imps disliked him very much. So they thought they would sell him the enchanted bellows.

"My bellows are broken," said Grunts. "I want a new pair. Show me some."

So the imps showed him a lot, and then they took out the enchanted pair. The ducks on the handle were beautifully carved, and Grunts liked them.

"How much are these?" he asked.

"Only a ha'penny," said Squeak. "The others are all a penny each."

"Then I'll take the ha'penny pair," said Grunts, and he put a bent and battered halfpenny down on the counter. Bubble wrapped the bellows up in brown paper, and gave them to the gnome.

Off he went, and the two imps looked at one another and laughed.

"Let's follow him and see what happens!" said Bubble, feeling very naughty indeed.

So they followed Grunts to his home in the bluebell wood. He lived not far away from the palace of the Fairy King and Queen, and had a very nice little cottage. He was one of the gardeners and kept the grounds of the palace in good order.

Now just as he had nearly reached his home, with

the imps close behind him, following quietly in his footsteps, someone came running to meet Grunts.

"The Queen wants you!" panted the messenger. "She wants some extra special roses for a dinner-party to-night, and says will you please pick them now?"

"I'll go straight to the palace," said Grunts. So, instead of going home, he turned to the right, and took the path that led to the palace garden. The imps went too, for they thought they would like to see the roses.

Grunts went in at a little green gate, and picked the roses for the Queen. Just as he had finished gathering a beautiful bunch, Her Majesty came down the path.

"Oh, thank you, Grunts," she said. "I'll take them in myself. Oh dear me, what's this?"

She had nearly fallen over the brown parcel in which the bellows were. Grunts had put it down on the grass whilst he picked the roses.

"I beg your pardon, Your Majesty," he said. "Those are my new bellows."

"Oh, *could* you lend me them for a moment?" asked the Queen. "The fire in the drawing-room wants a good blowing, and we can't find the bellows anywhere."

"Certainly, Your Majesty," said Grunts. "Pray let me come and do it for you,"

He picked up the bellows, and walked down the path with the Queen. The two imps were full of horror. Oh dear, oh dear! Whatever would happen in the palace when the bellows blew! They ran after the Queen and Grunts, meaning to beg them not to use the bellows.

But they were too late. Grunts was kneeling down by the fire, blowing hard with the bellows, when the two imps looked in at the window.

Then things began to happen. Suddenly a loud wheezing sound came from the bellows, and they leapt right out of Grunt's hands. They worked themselves, and a great wind came out of them. It blew all the roses out of the vase that the Queen had put them in. Then it blew all the newspapers out of the rack, and puffed the curtains right out of the window.

"Oh, oh!" cried the Queen. "Whatever is happening? Take the bellows outside, Grunts! There is something wrong with them!"

But Grunts couldn't catch them! They went flying all over the place, blowing for all they were worth. Puff-puff-puff! And off went the cushions from the couch and into the air went the tablecloth! The cat was blown right off her chair, and the dog sailed out of the room backwards. The Queen's lovely golden hair was blown all about her face, and she had to hold tightly to the mantlepiece to prevent herself from being blown out of the window!

"Ooh!" cried Bubble and Squeak as the bellows suddenly puffed at them. Off they went, blown backwards, rolling over and over. Then they sat up and looked at one another.

Bubble began to cry.

"I do wish we hadn't been naughty," he sobbed.

"Look what's happened now! Whoever would have thought that the Blowaway Witch would have sold us such a strong spell for sixpence. And it's getting stronger every minute!"

So it was. The bellows made a much louder noise now, and blew so strongly that even chairs and tables went rolling over. Then the bellows flew out into the hall, and met a footman carrying a tray of cups and plates. Every single one was blown into the air, and came down in pieces. As for the poor footman, he was blown to the end of the hall, and knocked over the King himself!

"Now what's this, what's this?" cried the King in a temper. "What do you mean by tearing about backwards like this, footman?"

But just then the bellows came near and—puff! The King himself was blown into the air and bumped his head against the ceiling. He caught hold of a swinging lantern, and hung there, very much frightened. The footman ran to get a ladder to help him down.

What a to-do there was in the palace! The King shouted, the Queen cried, the footman rushed here and there trying to catch the bellows. and the cook threw a saucepan at them, but only managed to hit the butler, who was very angry.

The bellows thoroughly enjoyed themselves. They sent a large bed sailing into the garden, and went out after it. Then they blew two chimney-pots off the roof, and puffed so hard at a gardener that he found himself sitting at the top of a beech tree before he knew what was happening.

Suddenly a loud wheezing sound came from the bellows, and they leapt right out of Grunts' hands.

Grunts was filled with amazement. How could his pair of bellows be so wicked? Hadn't he bought them for a ha'penny that day from Bubble and Squeak? Surely they couldn't have put such a strong spell into them?

As for Bubble and Squeak, they were shaking and trembling, for they knew that they would be found out and punished sooner or later. Whatever would the Queen say to them? And how could that dreadful pair of bellows be stopped?

"Let's run to the Blowaway Witch and ask her what to do!" said Bubble with tears running down his turned-up nose. So off they went.

They didn't stop once till they reached the Witch's cottage. Then they banged on her door.

When she came, they told her all that had happened.

"The King was blown up to the ceiling, and the gardener sailed up to the top of the beech tree, and all the cups and saucers and plates flew into the air off the footman's tray!" sobbed Bubble. "Oh, whatever are we to do? We didn't know you had given us such a strong wind-spell, witch. How can we stop it?"

The witch went very pale, and sat down suddenly.

"*I* didn't give you a strong spell," she said. "I gave you the weakest one I had, for I was afraid you were up to mischief, as usual. What *can* have happened to it?"

"Do you suppose the South Wind did anything to your spell?" asked Squeak. "He was here when you sold it to us, you know."

"So he was," said the witch, jumping up. "Well, I'll get him here, and ask him."

She took an old tea-tray out to her garden, and banged it with an iron spoon. In three minutes the South Wind came rushing down.

"What do you want?" he asked. "I heard you calling me."

The witch told him all that had happened at the palace, and the South Wind looked most uncomfortable.

"Yes," he said. "I breathed on the spell and made it very strong indeed—VERY strong indeed—but of course I hadn't any idea at all that the Queen herself would ask for the bellows to be used in the palace. I thought perhaps some old gnome or goblin would get a shock, that's all."

"Well, what are we to do?" asked the imps.

"I and the South Wind will come with you and see if we can stop the bellows from blowing," said the witch. She put on her best cloak, climbed on her broomstick, took the two imps behind her, and then set off with the South Wind to the palace.

When they arrived there, they found the enchanted bellows still blowing everywhere. The King's crown had been blown to the top of a chimney, and six hens had been puffed up to the highest tower of the palace. It was dreadful.

The witch hastily drew a circle of white chalk, and stepped inside it. Then she chanted a long string of magic words, beckoning the bellows towards her all the time. Little by little they stopped blowing, and came towards the witch. As soon as they were near the magic circle, she reached out her hand and grabbed them. Once they were in the circle all their enchantment left them, and they became ordinary bellows.

"Well, they're cured now," said the witch, and she stepped out of her circle. She went to the Queen and told her everything that had happened to make the bellows behave so strangely.

The King and Queen were very angry.

"The imps had no right to play tricks like that," they said, "and as for the South Wind, he ought to be ashamed of himself for his share in this terrible muddle. Just look at the palace! All upside down and topsy-turvy! He shall be banished from Fairyland for a whole year, and he can take those mischievous imps with him!"

Very sorrowfully the South Wind went away, and the two imps followed him, weeping bitterly. The footman picked up the bellows and threw them after the imps—and as soon as they left the magic circle, their enchantment came back. They began to blow and blow again, and the two imps flew straight up into the air, and found themselves in the clouds.

The South Wind caught the bellows, and gave them to the imps.

"I will look after you and be your friend," he said, "but you must work for me in return. Sometimes I can't be bothered to blow the clouds along on a summer's day, because I'm too sleepy. You can blow them for me with these bellows."

And that is what Bubble and Squeak do now. If you see the clouds sailing along on a summer's day when there is no breeze, you will be able to guess what is happening—the South Wind is fast asleep somewhere, and the two imps are puffing the clouds along with the bellows. They hope to go back to Fairyland some day, and if they are good, I expect they will.

The Talking Clock

Pooh and Penny were two little brownies who lived in Pooh-Penny Cottage at the end of Acorn Village. They were a mean and untruthful couple, and very few of the people in the village liked them. But they liked each other very well, for neither of them minded telling an untruth, and both were very good at taking things that didn't belong to them.

Now one day, when Pooh and Penny were walking along the road to Bumble-Bee Common, they heard a noise behind them. They turned round and saw that it was Farmer Tickles' big farm-cart, filled with furniture.

"Hey, are you moving?" cried Pooh.

"No," said Tickles; "the Wise Man, old Mr. Know-a-lot, has taken a house in the next village, and it's *his* things I'm moving. Good morning to you."

He drove on, and the cart jolted over a rut. Something fell out of the back. The two brownies looked to see if Farmer Tickles had noticed—but he hadn't.

"Wait till he's out of sight!" whispered Pooh to Penny. "Then we'll see what it is. If he's so careless as to lose things, it's his own fault."

Of course Pooh and Penny ought to have shouted after Farmer Tickles, but they were not going to do that—dear me no! They would keep whatever it was for themselves, the dishonest rogues.

Soon the cart turned a corner, and the two brownies ran to see what had fallen. It was something in a large parcel. Pooh snapped the string and Penny undid the paper.

"It's a big blue clock!" said Pooh. "Ooh, it's just what we want in the middle of our mantelpiece, Penny."

"But won't people see that it's the Wise Man's clock?" asked Penny.

"Not if we paint it red, instead of blue," said Pooh. So they took the clock home with them, and Pooh got some bright red paint and painted the blue clock red all over. It didn't look a bit the same when he had finished it. He put it in the middle of his mantelpiece and looked at it proudly.

"It isn't going," said Penny.

"I'll wind it up," said Pooh. So he wound it up carefully, and it said tick-tock, tick-tock, very slowly and solemnly. It struck the hours too, and chimed ding-dong-ding-dong. Pooh and Penny were delighted.

Now that afternoon the landlord, Mr. Chuff-chuff, came for his rent. The brownies asked him in and then pulled a very long face. They hated paying their rent, and always got out of it if they could.

"We're sorry, Chuff-chuff, but we have had a dreadful lot of expenses lately," began Pooh, "and we haven't any money to give you this time."

"We're really *very* sorry," said Penny, looking as if he were about to cry. "We wondered if you could possibly let us off this time."

Mr. Chuff-chuff was a very kind-hearted man, and he looked quite sorry for Pooh and Penny. He didn't guess that they really had plenty of money hidden away, and were just trying to cheat him because of his kind heart.

"Well," he said, "I'm sorry to hear of your troubles, Pooh and Penny. Perhaps I'd better let you off this time, and then——"

But something made him stop. It was a funny little voice coming from he didn't know where, and this is what it said:

"Ooh, the story-tellers! Ooh, the fibbers! Why, they've got a whole bag of gold hidden up the chimney! You go and look, Chuff-chuff!"

Pooh and Penny stared at one another with their mouths wide open. Each thought the other had spoken. Both felt very angry, and they boxed one another's ears hard.

Chuff-chuff let them fight. He went to the chimney and looked up. Sure enough there was a bag on the ledge there. He pulled it down and looked inside. It was full of gold!

"You horrid, mean little brownies!" he cried. "You thought that if you told a story to me, my kind heart would say you needn't pay me my money. Well, there's plenty here, so I shall take what you owe me!"

And he did! He walked out of Pooh-Penny Cottage with five gold pieces, and the two brownies were as angry as angry could be.

"Why did you tell him where our gold was?" asked Pooh angrily.

"I didn't!" said Penny. "It must have been you. You *are* silly!"

"I tell you it wasn't!" shouted Pooh, and he pinched Penny's arm very hard and made him squeal.

Then Penny punched Pooh, and goodness knows how long they would have gone on doing that if there hadn't come another knock at the door.

Pooh opened it. Kind old Mother Bonny stood outside.

"I've come to see if you'll lend me an umbrella just to pop across the road," she said. "It's pouring with rain and I shall get soaked. I'll bring it back at once."

Pooh and Penny hated lending anything. They shook their heads.

"We're sorry," said Pooh, "but our only umbrella is broken, and has gone to be mended."

"Ooh, the story-tellers! Ooh, the fibbers!" cried a funny little voice from somewhere. "If that isn't an umbrella standing over there in the corner, and a brand-new one too!"

Mother Bonny looked into the corner, and sure enough there stood a fine new umbrella. She looked at Pooh and Penny in scorn.

"So you wouldn't even lend a neighbour your umbrella!" she said. "Well, you're meaner than I thought! I shan't ask *you* to my party this summer!"

She slammed the door and went out into the rain. Pooh and Penny stared at one another.

"Did *you* say that about a brand new umbrella in the corner?" Pooh asked Penny.

"Of course not!" said Penny. "I believe *you* did! You *are* stupid!"

"Ho, I'm stupid, am I!" cried Pooh in a rage. "Well, take that!"

He boxed Penny's ears, and the two began to fight again.

"Ha, ha!" cried a funny little voice. "Ho ho! What a fine sight to see two nasty little brownies smacking one another!"

Pooh and Penny stopped fighting and looked round.

"Then it *wasn't* you talking!" they each cried to the other. "Who is it?"

"Let's look and see," said Pooh. "There must be someone hiding in our kitchen."

Well, they looked everywhere, but they could find no one at all. They opened the larder door, they looked under the table and they peeped up the chimney—but there was no one in Pooh-Penny Cottage except themselves.

"Well, this is very queer," said Pooh at last, sitting down. "There was certainly a voice speaking, but who can it belong to?"

"It belongs to *me*," said the funny little voice again.

Pooh and Penny jumped. They looked all round, but still they couldn't see anyone.

"Where are you?" asked Penny, feeling a bit frightened.

"Ha ha!" said the voice. "I'm on the mantelpiece, and I've a very good view of everything, I can tell you!"

Pooh and Penny looked at the mantelpiece, but there was no one there.

"Don't tell stories!" said Pooh, crossly. "There's no one on the mantelpiece at all! There's only a red clock, a tea-caddy and a blue jar."

"Well, I'm the red clock!" said the little voice with a chuckle. "I *used* to be blue, but now I'm red, and perhaps you'd be good enough to tell me why you painted me another colour?"

Pooh and Penny turned pale. They stared at the clock in dismay. A talking clock! What a surprising thing! They didn't like it at all. It looked quite ordinary—but no, as they watched it, they saw it had a queer little face of its own, and it winked and blinked at them as they looked at it.

"Well, you'll know me the next time," said the clock, cheekily. "How you do stare, to be sure! This is a nice kitchen you've got, and I like this mantelpiece, I've such a good view of everything."

"Pooh!" whispered Penny. "We can't keep that horrid clock. It will give all our secrets away. Let's get a hammer, take it out into the yard and smash it to bits."

"All right," said Pooh. So they found their hammer, picked up the clock and took it into the yard. Pooh put the clock on the ground and Penny brought the hammer down on it with all his might.

Smash! The hammer flew into a hundred bits—but the clock hadn't even a dent in it! Pooh and Penny stared in fright.

"Ha ha, ho ho!" laughed the clock, loudly. "You can't kill me! I'm a magic clock, I am. See what's happened to your hammer! Oh, what a joke! Well, I'm going back to your mantelpiece, if you don't mind!"

And with that the astonishing clock grew a pair of spindly legs, ran back into the cottage, leapt on to the mantelpiece and stood there, ticking away merrily.

"This is awful," said Pooh and Penny. "We *must* get rid of it *some*how. Perhaps to-night, when everyone is asleep, we can think of some way of destroying it."

Just then someone tapped at the door of the kitchen, and Old Dame Trips looked in.

"Have you any eggs for sale?" she asked. "I'm making cakes and I've run short of eggs. Can you let me have six?"

"Certainly," said Pooh, and he went into the

larder and got six eggs from the shelf. "That will be sixpence, Dame Trips."

"You're sure they're new-laid?" asked the old dame. "I don't want to spoil my cakes with bad eggs, you know."

"Oh they were only laid this morning," said Pooh, which was a dreadful story, for they were at least five weeks old.

"Ooh, the story-teller! Ooh, the fibber!" cried the clock, in a loud voice. "They're no more new-laid than I am! You go and buy your eggs from the bee-woman over the way, Dame Trips. They're fresh and new."

"Well, I never!" cried Dame Trips in astonishment, looking round to see who had spoken. She was more astonished than ever when she could see no one. "Pooh and Penny, what does this mean? Aren't these eggs really new-laid?"

Pooh and Penny blushed red, and didn't answer a word. They were so afraid that the clock would say something even worse if they told another story.

Dame Trips took a basin and broke one of the eggs into it. Oh, the dreadful smell that came from it!

"It's as bad as an egg can be!" she cried. "Oh, you wicked little brownies, to think of selling me such dreadful eggs! Why, you'd have spoilt all my cakes."

And, oh dear me, the angry old dame picked up the basin and emptied the bad egg all over the two brownies! Then out she went and banged the door in a temper.

Pooh and Penny wiped the egg off their heads, and glared at the clock, which was laughing till tears ran down its shining glass face. Then Pooh picked up one of the bad eggs and aimed carefully at the chuckling clock. He threw the egg at it with all his might—but the clock skipped to one side and there was the nice clean mirror behind dripping with bad egg!

"Try again, try again!" cried the clock in glee.

Penny picked up *two* eggs and hurled them at the clock, but, oh my, what a bad shot he was! He struck the pretty blue jar, and knocked it off the mantelpiece. It crashed to pieces in the fireplace below.

Then in a rage Pooh picked up the last two eggs and flung them straight at the clock, but somehow or other they hit the tea-caddy, and that flew right off the mantelpiece and spilt all the tea on the hearth-rug! How the clock laughed! How it danced and skipped on its little spindly legs!

Pooh and Penny cried with rage. They got a cloth and wiped up all the mess. The eggs smelt terrible, and made them feel quite ill. They picked up the pieces of the blue jar and put them into the dust-bin, and then they swept up the tea-leaves, groaning to see what a lot of good tea was wasted.

"Let's wait till night comes," whispered Pooh. So they waited and did nothing till darkness fell. Then when one by one the lights in Acorn Village went out, the two brownies picked up the clock again, and stole out-of-doors to the pond that lay in the middle of the village. They meant to drown the clock!

As soon as they reached the water they threw the clock right into the middle—but oh, my goodness, how it shouted!

"Help! Help!" it cried. "Help! I'm drowning!"

At once lights went on in all the cottages round and folk came rushing out. They saw Pooh and Penny standing by the pond, and they called out to them to know what had happened.

"Nothing," said the brownies. "It must be someone having a joke. There's no one in the pond at all."

"Ooh, the story-tellers! Ooh, the fibbers!" cried the struggling clock. "I'm drowning, I tell you! Pooh and Penny threw me in the water to drown me!"

"Oh the wicked brownies!" cried everyone, and they caught hold of Pooh and Penny before they could run away. "Get a stick and help the poor drowning person out of the water!"

A long stick was brought, and soon the clock managed to catch hold of it with its two spindly legs.

"Pull me in, pull me in!" he cried. The people pulled him in—and goodness gracious, they couldn't believe their eyes when they saw that it wasn't a live person at all, but a big red clock!

"This is strange!" they said. "Clock, who do you belong to? And why are Pooh and Penny trying to drown you?"

"I belong to the Wise Man, Know-a-lot," said

the shivering clock. "I fell off the cart and Pooh and Penny picked me up and took me home, though they knew quite well I belonged to someone else. Well, I'm a talking clock, you know, and as soon as I saw what dreadful stories these two mean and dishonest brownies told to everyone who came to the door, I just spoke out."

"Go on, go on!" cried the listening people.

"Well, Pooh and Penny didn't like that," said the clock. "So first they tried to smash me with a hammer, then they tried to hit me with bad eggs, and now they've tried to drown me!"

"The wicked rogues!" cried everyone. "We'll put them in prison for to-night, and to-morrow we'll take them to the Wise Man and tell him all about them!"

So they took Pooh and Penny to the police-station and locked them up for the night. Then they dried the clock, and Mr. Chuff-chuff took it home and put it on his mantelpiece for the night.

In the morning all the folk of Acorn Village took the two brownies and the clock to the Wise Man in the next village. He was most astonished to see such a crowd coming.

"You can't all come into my small cottage," he said. "Let's sit in the garden and I'll hear what you have to say."

So everyone sat down except Pooh and Penny, who were made to stand up. Then Mr. Chuff-chuff told all that had happened, and the Wise Man listened gravely.

"This is a dreadful thing," he said, when Chuff-

chuff had finished. "Pooh and Penny must certainly be punished."

"They must!" shouted everyone.

"But how?" asked Chuff-chuff.

"I think we'll let the clock punish them!" said the Wise Man, with a sly smile. "I won't take it back, I'll let Pooh and Penny have it for their own. It shall stand on their mantelpiece and say whatever it likes! Then, whenever they tell a story or do a mean thing everyone will know!"

"Good idea!" cried all the folk in delight. "Oh, what fun! We shall always know now when the brownies are not being truthful!"

"And, since Pooh and Penny caused you all to be awakened in the middle of the night and to lose some of your sleep, they shall each get one spank from all of you," said the Wise Man. "That will teach them not to try to drown clocks again!"

How Pooh and Penny sobbed and cried, but it wasn't a bit of good. Each one of the people from Acorn Village gave them one good spank. Then they all marched home with the two brownies and the clock, and put it right in the very middle of the mantelpiece again.

"There!" they said. "The clock will look after you all right, Pooh and Penny! You can't deceive us any more!"

What fun that clock had! It was always on the watch to correct the brownies when they told a story, and it never missed a single chance of telling them when they were mean or deceitful. Soon the two brownies hardly dared to say a word.

"Is there *any* way of making you be quiet?" Pooh asked the clock one night, in despair.

"Oh, yes," said the clock. "If you tell the truth, and act kindly and faithfully towards others, I should never say a word again! But goodness me, you'll never stop *my* tongue—you're too bad, both of you!"

In bed that night Pooh and Penny talked over what the clock had said.

"Look here, Pooh, let's try to tell the truth and be kind just for a week," said Penny. "Let's see if that nasty old clock will keep quiet. I'm tired of everyone laughing at us."

So for a whole week Pooh and Penny spoke nothing but the truth, and tried to be really kind—and will you believe it, the clock said never a word from Monday to Sunday!

"Well, we've done it!" said Penny, when Sunday came. "That old clock hasn't been able to open its mouth once! And I say, Pooh—I *liked* speaking the truth and being kind—didn't you? It made me feel so nice and clean."

"Yes, I felt the same," said Pooh, blushing red. "Penny, we *have* been horrid little brownies. No wonder everyone disliked us, and no one would be friends. Shall we try *always* to be good and kind?"

"Let's!" said Penny, and they shook hands solemnly on that promise.

Well, it was very hard at first to forget their old bad ways, and sometimes the clock found its voice again—but after a while the brownies found it easier to tell the truth than to tell stories, and when once they had found how lovely it was to be kind and loving, they were never mean or unkind again.

"You *are* changed!" said Mr. Chuff-chuff, next time he called for his rent. "Why, you're as nice a pair of brownies now as ever I've seen! I'm pleased to know you! That clock must be getting tired of sitting on your mantelpiece doing nothing!"

Then the clock spoke for the last time.

"Yes," it said, in its funny little voice, "I *am* tired of being here, never getting a chance to say a word all day! I'm going! Good-bye!"

And it suddenly grew its two spindly little legs again, leapt off the mantelpiece and ran out of the door. The brownies and Chuff-chuff watched it running down the street, but where it went to nobody knows.

I only hope it never comes and sits on *your* mantelpiece! You must be careful how you behave if it does!

The Goblin House

MOLLY and Jim were out for a walk in the woods. They had taken their tea with them but it wasn't much of a tea—just two pieces of rather dry bread, and half an apple each.

"I do wish Daddy could get some work to do," said Molly. "Mummy is getting so worried, and I know she doesn't have enough to eat. She gives everything to us, and says she isn't hungry."

"Daddy's so clever too," said Jim. "He can make every kind of key there is, and I'm sure there isn't a lock or catch anywhere that he couldn't mend if it was broken."

"Where shall we have our tea?" asked Molly. "Shall we have it here, or go a bit farther on?"

"Let's go on," said Jim. "Look, here's a dear little path that we've never been down before."

They went down the path for some way, and then stopped and listened. They could hear little high voices somewhere nearby. Who could it be?

The children peeped round a tree, and then saw the funniest sight! There was a queer little higgledy-piggledy house set in a little clearing. It was red and yellow, with funny small round windows. All round it, looking about them in the grass, were twelve small goblins, talking to each other in high voices.

"Goblins!" whispered Jim in astonishment. "They're looking for something."

"Aren't they queer!" said Molly. "Do let's go and speak to them, Jim. They won't do us any harm, I'm sure."

So they walked out from behind their tree, and went up to the goblins, who seemed most surprised to see them. They all ran together in a bunch, and stared at Molly and Jim.

"Have you lost anything?" asked Molly, in a kind voice.

"Yes," said the biggest goblin. "We've lost the key of our little house, and we can't get in until we find it. My wife and all my ten children have been helping me to look for it for two hours, but we can't find it anywhere!"

"Oh dear, what a pity!" said Molly. "We'll help you to look, if you like."

So the two children began to hunt about the grass for the key, but they couldn't find it anywhere. The goblins were very much upset, and two of the smallest ones began to cry. Molly couldn't help staring at them in astonishment because the tears that rolled down their brown cheeks were bright green.

"We shall have to spend the night out of doors," said the father goblin, sadly. "I only hope the children won't catch cold."

Then Jim had a splendid idea.

"I say!" he said. "My Daddy is a locksmith—you know, he makes keys and things like that. He has about a thousand odd ones in his workshop. Shall I go home and ask him to let me bring the smallest ones here, and see if any of them fit your little house? If we can find a key that fits, I'm sure my Daddy will give it to you."

The goblins were delighted, and they all crowded round Jim, and thanked him. He and Molly ran back home as fast as they could, and found their daddy in his workshop.

"Daddy, there's a little goblin house in the wood, and the goblins have lost its key, so they can't get in," began Jim breathlessly. "Could you let me take some of your tiniest keys to them just to see if any will fit?"

"Goblins!" said Daddy, laughing. "Don't be silly, Jim."

"I'm not," said Jim. "I expect it's hard for you to believe in goblins, Daddy, because you're grown-up, but anyhow, may I take the keys?"

"Yes, if you like," said Daddy, still laughing. So Molly and Jim hurriedly looked through all the different keys that lay on the shelves. They chose the very smallest, for they knew that it would have to be a very tiny key to fit such a small lock as that on the goblin's door.

Jim put them into a bag, and together the children ran off again. They took the same path, and soon arrived at the goblin house, where they found all the goblins patiently waiting.

Jim gave the father goblin the bag of keys, and one by one he tried to fit them into the lock. But alas! Either the key was too big, or if it fitted, it wouldn't turn. All the little goblins watched breathlessly, and Mrs. Goblin breathed so hard down Jim's neck that it tickled him.

And then they tried a queer little key that slipped in beautifully. The goblin turned it, and there was a click! The door was unlocked! It opened, and all the goblins crowded in, shouting in delight. Jim and Molly were as excited as they were.

"Please come in," said Mrs. Goblin to the children. "We shall all have tea now, and we would be so pleased if you would have some with us. If you hadn't helped us, we would have had to go without tea and supper and beds and everything!"

So Jim and Molly stayed to tea with the goblins. It was the queerest, loveliest tea they had ever had. There were cakes made like flowers, and jellies shaped like birds. There was wild strawberry jam and honey tea. The children ate and ate and ate, and so did the little goblins, for they told Jim and Molly that they had had no dinner, because of their key being lost.

"Please keep the key," said Jim. "My Daddy

won't ever want it again. And if I were you, I'd tie a string to it, and fasten the other end of the string to your belt—then you won't ever lose it again."

The goblins thought that was a simply wonderful idea, and they did it at once. Then the father goblin pulled out a tiny purse.

"I'd like to pay you for your kindness," he said.

"Oh, *no*!" said Jim and Molly, together. "We don't want to be paid—and besides, Mummy says we must never take money for helping people. She says we must help people for kindness and nothing else."

"What a nice mother you've got," said the goblin, admiringly. "Have you got a nice father too?"

"Oh, yes," said Molly. "But he's very worried just now because he can't get any work to do. Nobody seems to want keys or padlocks or doors mended or anything like that, and he can't earn any money."

"Dear me," said the goblin, kindly. "Well, we'll see that he has plenty of work to do in future."

Molly and Jim didn't quite see how goblins could bring their father work, but they were too polite to say so—so they said good-bye, thanked Mrs. Goblin for her lovely tea, and then ran off. They told their father and mother all about their adventures, but neither of them seemed to believe their story.

Next morning, all sorts of people came running to the children's father, asking him to come and do some work for them.

"Our window catches have all gone wrong," said one. "We want you to mend them."

"The locks on all our doors have jammed," said another. "It really is a most extraordinary thing—we had to climb out of the window this morning, because we couldn't open any of the doors. Please come as soon as you can, and get them right for us."

"We've lost all our keys," said another. "Someone must have taken them in the night. Will you bring us new locks and keys as soon as you can?"

The children's father was most astonished. The children looked at each other, and then spoke together.

"It's the goblins! They said they would see that you had plenty of work, Daddy! They must have been up to mischief in the night, so that people would come to ask your help in the morning."

"Nonsense!" said Daddy. "I don't believe in those goblins of yours!"

The children ran out into the garden.

"Of course, it's lovely for Daddy to get all this work," said Jim, "but it's not right to go and fiddle with other people's things, is it, Molly? I don't think the goblins ought to do that."

"No, they oughtn't," said Molly. "But perhaps they don't know the difference between right and wrong, as we do. Shall we go and tell them they mustn't go round and make things go wrong?"

"Yes," said Jim. "It's kind of them to want to help us, but they mustn't do it that way."

So off they went and once more took the little path that led to the goblin house. But when they got to where it had stood the day before—it wasn't there!

"Isn't that queer!" cried Jim, walking all around, trying to puzzle out what had happened. But he couldn't. The goblin house had completely disappeared.

"Well, we can't tell them what we came to say," said Molly. "Still, perhaps they won't meddle with other people's locks and keys any more."

They didn't, you'll be glad to know—but everyone was so pleased with the quick, clever way in which the children's father mended all the things that had suddenly gone wrong, that he was never out of work again, and Molly and Jim were very happy.

They often go to the place where they found the goblin house, but they have never seen it again, nor have they seen the little goblins. But if ever you see a goblin with a key tied to his belt, you'll know who he is, and you'll probably find his house somewhere round about!

The Flying Goat

ONCE upon a time a great fair came to the village of Penny-come-quick. There were round-abouts, swings, coco-nut shies, conjurers, clowns, and a score of other splendid things. Little Benny Biggles was so excited that he couldn't sleep for thinking of it all.

He went every single day, and of all the wonderful things at the fair there was one that he simply couldn't take his eyes off. This was a wooden goat with wings on each of its heels.

A Chinaman had charge of it, and if anyone paid a sixpence he would make the goat rise into the air, fly round the fair-ground and then come back again to him. Benny could have watched that all day. He thought it was the most wonderful thing he had ever seen.

"I wonder how it does it?" he said to himself. "Wouldn't I love to ride on it!"

Now no sooner did he think that than his heart began to beat very fast indeed. Why *shouldn't* he have a ride on the goat?

"I'll just see if I can!" said Benny. So the next day, when the Chinaman was taking sixpences, Benny stood as close to him as he could to see what he did to make the goat fly off.

"It's easy!" said Benny to himself. "Why, he just pulls one ear back, that's all! I could do that myself!"

When the Chinaman's back was turned, and he was telling everyone about his wonderful goat, Benny crept up to it.

"My goat, he will fly all round the fair," said the man. "Give me just one more sixpence and you shall see him go!"

Benny suddenly leapt on the goat's back. All the people cried out "Oh!" in surprise, and the Chinaman turned round quickly. When he saw Benny on his goat, he ran towards him, shouting out something in a strange language that the boy could not understand.

But before he could get to the goat, Benny pulled back its right ear. In a second the wooden creature rose into the air, all its foot-wings flapping hard. Benny hung on tightly, his breath taken away.

"Ooh!" he cried. "What an adventure! Go on, goat, go on!"

The goat flew right round the fair-ground, and Benny could see everyone below staring up at him in the greatest astonishment. The people pointed their fingers at him, and shouted to one another.

"See! A little boy is riding the enchanted goat!" they cried.

Benny expected the goat to fly down to the Chinaman after it had gone round the fair-ground once, for that was what it always did.

But oh dear me! The goat didn't go down to the Chinaman! After it had circled round the ground once, it suddenly rose much higher in the air, and started flying straight towards the setting sun! Benny was too surprised to say anything at first, and then he gave a shout.

"Hie! Hie! You're going the wrong way, goat! Take me back to the fair-ground! Hurry up and turn round!"

But the goat took no notice of Benny at all. It went on flying towards the sun, very fast and very straight. Benny began to feel frightened. He clung on tightly, his hair streaming out behind him. Below him he could see fields and hills stretched out very small, like a toy countryside. He saw a train going along a railway line, and it seemed to him to be smaller even than his own clockwork train at home.

"Stop! Stop!" he shouted to the goat. "You are taking me too far! Turn round and go back to the fair!"

Still the goat took no notice. Benny kicked its wooden sides with his feet, but that didn't do any good either. Whatever was he to do?

On and on went the goat, faster than ever. Soon

they came to the sea. When they were right over it, the little boy looked downwards. He saw dark blue water stretching out all around him. No land was in sight at all. Benny had no idea that the sea was so big. He clutched the goat more tightly, afraid that he would fall into the water far below.

The sun sank down into the western sky and darkness came. The stars twinkled brightly, the moon came up, and Benny grew very sleepy. He began to cry, for he was afraid.

"I wish I knew how to stop this goat," he sobbed. "I expect it will go on like this for ever and ever, and I'll go round and round the world till I fall off."

Then he dried his tears and began to think hard.

"If I pull the right ear back to start the goat, perhaps I push it *forward* to stop it," he thought. But before he did anything, he peeped downwards to see if they were over land or sea. They were still flying over the water, but Benny could see an island not far off. He decided to try and land on that.

He pushed the goat's right ear forward. Nothing happened at all. The goat still went steadily on. Then the little boy took hold of the *left* ear, and pulled that back. At once the goat began to slow down!

"I've found the secret, I've found the secret!" cried Benny in delight. "Oh, if only I'd thought of that before!"

He peered below him, and saw that the goat had not quite reached the island, but would land in the water round it. So he quickly pushed the left ear forward again, and pulled the right ear back. The goat at once flew straight onwards. When he was exactly over the island, Benny pushed the right ear forward and pulled the left ear back.

The goat flew down to the land. Benny tried to see what it was like, but except that he thought he could make out a huge building of some sort, he could see little. Nearer and nearer to the land came the goat, and at last it was skimming only a few feet above the ground. Then bump! It landed, and stood quite still while Benny got off.

The little boy saw that he was at the edge of a wood, but it was so dark that he knew it was no use trying to find anyone to help him. He must wait till the morning. He stretched his stiff legs, and yawned, for it was long past his bedtime, and he was very sleepy.

Then he felt for the goat's ears. He carefully pushed the left ear forward, and made certain that the right ear was in its proper position too. Then he found a patch of heather, and curling up in it, he fell fast asleep.

It was day when he awoke, and the sun was shining in the eastern sky. Benny looked around him in surprise, for at first he did not remember how he had come there. Then he saw the wooden goat standing nearby, and he remembered everything.

"Ooh, I *am* hungry!" he said, jumping to his feet. "I wonder where I can get something to eat. Then I'll jump on to my old goat and go off home. If I fly to the east, I'm sure to get there sometime. As soon as I see the fair-ground beneath me. I shall fly down to it!"

He looked round him. He could hear the sound of the sea nearby, and he remembered that he was on an island. Behind him was a wood, and to the right was a very high hill—almost a mountain. On the very top was an enormous castle with thousands of glittering windows.

"Good gracious!" said Benny in astonishment. "Whoever lives there?"

He saw a smaller hill nearby, and after carefully hiding the wooden goat under a bush, he started off to go to the top. When he stood on the summit he looked around him. He saw sea on every side, for the island was quite small. It had two hills, the one he was on, and the very high one on which the castle stood. A little wood lay between and from the very middle of it rose some smoke.

"Someone must live there," said Benny. "I'll go and ask them if they would kindly give me something to eat, for I've never been so hungry in all my life before!"

Down the hill he went, and into the wood. He soon found a little path, and followed it. After a while he came to the queerest house he had ever seen. It was quite small, and was built of precious stones glittering so brightly that Benny was almost dazzled. Round it was a circle of white stones.

Benny walked up to the circle. He stood outside, trying to see the door of the cottage—but he could see none, though he walked all round it several times.

"Well, I'll just have to go right up and see where it is," said the little boy. So he put his foot over the ring of white stones to walk up to the house. But good gracious me! He couldn't put it to the ground again! It was held there in the air, though Benny could not see anyone or anything holding it. Then all at once there came the noise of a hundred trumpets blowing and a thousand bells ringing!

"Oh my! Oh my!" said poor Benny. "This must be a magic circle or something!"

Suddenly there came a voice from the house. Benny looked, and saw a gnome's head peeping out of a window.

"Who are you?" demanded the gnome. "You have put your foot in my magic circle, and started all my bells ringing and trumpets blowing. Take your foot out."

Benny tried to but he couldn't.

"I can't," he said. "Please undo the spell or whatever it is. I'm getting so tired of standing on one leg. I'm only a little boy coming to ask for something to eat."

"Say your sixteen times table then," said the gnome sternly.

"Oh, I can't," said Benny, nearly crying. "Why, I'm only up to seven times at school, and I don't know *that* very well yet."

"Oh, that's all right then," said the gnome, smiling. "I thought you were a wizard or a witch disguised as a little boy. If you had been, you would have known your sixteen times table, but as you don't, I know you are a little boy. I've taken the spell off now. You can come into the magic circle."

Benny's foot was suddenly free. He stepped over the ring of white stones, and went up to the glittering house. He looked everywhere for a door, but he couldn't find one.

"Clap your hands twice, and call out 'open, open' seven times!" said the gnome.

Benny did so, and at once a door appeared in the wall and opened itself in front of him. The gnome looked out and pulled Benny inside by the hand. At once the door disappeared again.

"Why do all these things happen like this?" said Benny, puzzled. "Am I in Fairyland?"

"Not exactly," said the gnome, setting a big bowl of bread and milk in front of Benny. "This island was once part of Fairyland—just the two hills and the wood, you know—and a great giant came and built his castle on the top of the biggest hill."

"I thought giants weren't allowed in Fairyland," said Benny in astonishment.

"They're not," said the gnome, putting a hot cup of cocoa by Benny's side, "but this one was very cunning. He turned himself into a small goblin, and built a tiny castle. Nobody minded, of course, for there are lots of goblins in Fairyland. But one night he changed himself back to his proper shape, a giant as tall as a house, and made his castle grow big, too! What do you think of that?"

"Go on!" said Benny, eating his bread and milk. "This is very exciting!"

"Well, the giant was so big and so powerful that

the King and Queen couldn't get rid of him," said the gnome. "He was a terrible nuisance, because he would keep capturing fairies, and taking them to his castle. Then he would charge the King a thousand pieces of gold to get them back again."

"The horrid monster!" said Benny.

"Then as they couldn't make the giant go away," said the gnome, "they suddenly thought of putting a spell on the land he owned, and sending him away to the middle of the sea to become an island! So they did that, and off went the two hills and the wood one fine starlit night! They landed in the sea miles away with a terrible splash, and here we are!"

"But how did *you* come to be here?" asked Benny, puzzled.

"Well, I happened to have built my house in the wood without anyone knowing," said the gnome, sighing. "So of course, I went too, and I can't get back. The giant was in a terrible temper when he found what had happened. He came tearing down to me, and if I hadn't quickly put a spell round my house, he would certainly have turned me into a hedgehog or something like that."

"And does he live here all alone?" asked Benny.

"No, he has got seven fairies with him," said the gnome. "The King didn't know that he had stolen them on the very night his castle was moved, so of course the poor things are still there. I wish I could rescue them, but there is such a powerful spell round the castle that I couldn't get near it even if I tried all day!"

"What does he do with the fairies!" asked Benny, finishing his bread and milk to the very last crumb.

"They are his servants," said the gnome, "and very hard he makes them work, I can tell you. If they are not quick enough for him, he beats them, and I have often heard them crying, poor things. But they will never be rescued, for no one can get to the castle."

"What a shame!" said Benny. "Oh, how I wish *I* could rescue them!"

"You're only a little boy," said the gnome scornfully, "you couldn't possibly do anything."

Benny looked at the gnome. Then an idea flashed into his head.

"Tell me, Mister Gnome," he said, "is there a spell on the castle top as well as all around the walls?"

"Of course not!" said the gnome, staring at Benny in surprise. "The castle is much too high for anyone to get on the top. Why do you ask?"

"Because I think I *can* rescue the fairies!" said Benny, his heart beating very fast. "I've got an enchanted goat here, that I came on, and I believe I could make it fly to the castle-roof, and then, if I could only find the fairies quickly, they could mount on its back and I could take them away with me!"

"An enchanted goat!" said the gnome in astonishment, "then you're not a little boy after all. I'll put a spell on you if you're a witch or a wizard!"

"No, no, don't!" cried Benny, "I really *am* a boy. Listen and I'll tell you how I came here."

In a few minutes the gnome knew Benny's story. The little boy took him to where he had hidden the goat, and the gnome grew tremendously excited.

"Oh, Benny!" he cried, "I believe we'll do it! Oh, how grand!"

"Will you come with me?" asked Benny, "I feel a bit frightened all alone."

"Of course I will!" said the gnome. Then he and Benny got on to the goat's back, Benny pulled the right ear back, and off they went. They flew high above the castle, and then Benny made the goat go downwards. One part of this castle had a flat roof, and it was quite easy to land there.

"Talk in whispers now," said the gnome. "If the giant hears us, we shall be captured at once. Look! there are some steps going down from the roof. You'd better go down them, and see if you can find any of the fairies. I'll wait here."

Benny ran to the steps. He climbed down them very carefully. They went round and round and down and down. At last he came to the end and found himself in a long passage with doors opening off.

"Oh, dear! Had I better try each one to see if the fairies are inside?" thought Benny. "No, I won't; I'll go on to those stairs over there, and go down a bit farther. If the fairies do the work for the giant, they may be in the kitchen."

He went down some more stairs, and then down some more. They seemed to be never-ending. At last he heard a tremendous noise. It came from a room nearby. The door was open, and Benny peeped in. He saw an enormous giant lying in the biggest armchair he had ever seen. He was fast asleep, and the great noise Benny had heard was the giant snoring.

"Oh, good!" though Benny in delight. "Now I can look about in safety for the fairies."

He came to a smaller door, and listened. He thought he could hear the murmur of little voices behind, and he opened the door. Yes, he was right! Sitting round a big fire, polishing enormous mugs and dishes, was a group of small fairies. One of them was crying.

When the door opened, they all sprang to their feet expecting to see the giant. When they saw Benny, they were so astonished that none of them could speak a word.

"Sh! Sh!" said Benny, "I've come to rescue you! I've got an enchanted goat up on the roof. Hurry up and come along with me. I'll take you back to Fairyland."

The fairies were so full of joy that they ran to Benny and hugged him. Then they ran lightly out of the room and up the stairs, treading very softly indeed when they passed the room where the giant slept. Benny followed them, and at last they all reached the roof. The gnome stood there with the goat, and greeted them in delight.

How they hugged one another and smiled for joy! Two of the fairies wept for gladness and Benny had to lend them his handkerchief.

"Come on," said the gnome, at last. "We mustn't stop here. If the giant wakes he will be sure to miss you and put a spell on you somehow. Are you all here?"

Benny counted the fairies.

"Good gracious!" he said in dismay. "There are only six of them! Didn't you say there were seven, Mister Gnome?"

"Oh, where's Tiptoe, where's Tiptoe?" cried all the other fairies. "We've left her behind! She was watering the plants in the greenhouse, and we've left her behind!"

"Well, call her," said the gnome. "If the giant wakes it can't be helped. I expect she will get up here before he knows there is anything the matter."

So all together the fairies called.

"Tiptoe! Tiptoe! Come up to the roof at once! Tiptoe!"

A little voice from far below them answered them.

"I'm coming!"

Then suddenly there came a thunderous roar. The giant had woken up!

"WHO'S THAT CALLING?" he shouted. "YOU'VE WAKENED ME FROM MY SLEEP, YOU WICKED FAIRIES! I'LL PUNISH YOU, I WILL!"

"Ooh!" said the fairies, turning pale.

"It's all right," said the gnome. "By the time he's looked into the kitchen and called for you a few times, we shall be gone! Look, here's Tiptoe!"

The seventh fairy came running up the steps to the roof. In a trice the others explained everything to her.

"Get on the goat," said the gnome, "the giant is getting very angry indeed."

The fairies began to clamber on the goat—but whatever do you think! There was only room for five of them! The goat was much too small.

"Oh my, oh my!" groaned the gnome. "I don't think I've time to make it big enough for us all, but I'll try. Stand away everyone."

He drew a chalk ring round the goat, clapped his hands, and began to dance round and round it, singing a magic song. Little by little the wooden creature grew bigger.

The giant below was roaring more angrily than ever—and then Benny suddenly heard his footsteps coming up the stairs!

"Quick, quick, he's coming!" he shouted. The gnome hastily rubbed out the chalk circle with his foot, and ran to the goat. He pushed Benny on first and then helped all the fairies on. Last of all he got on himself, though there was really hardly room for him. Just as they were all on, the giant appeared at the opening of the roof.

Benny pulled back the right ear of the goat and at once the animal rose into the air. The giant gave a tremendous roar of anger and surprise, and fell down the steps in astonishment. By the time he had picked himself up, and was ready to work a powerful spell on the goat to bring it back, it was far away in the sky.

Benny was trembling with excitement, and so were all the others. For a long while no one spoke. Then the fairies all began to talk at once, and thanked Benny and the gnome over and over again for rescuing them. Benny listened to their little high voices, and thought them the sweetest sound he had ever heard.

After a long time he looked below him. To his great astonishment he was just over his own home! Away to the right was the fair-ground, and the music of the roundabouts came faintly to Benny's ears.

"Oh, I think I'll go down here," said Benny. "There's my home, and I *would* like to see my mother and tell her I'm all right. Do you mind if I get off here? The gnome will take you safely back to Fairyland."

So down they all went, and Benny jumped off the goat at the end of his own garden.

"Good-bye," he said. "And would you mind sending the goat back to the Chinaman at the fair? I expect he will be upset not to have it."

"Certainly," said the gnome, "we can easily do that. Well, thank you for all your help, Benny. Good-bye!"

"Good-bye, good-bye!" called the fairies, as the goat once more rose into the air. Benny watched them until he could no longer see them, and then ran indoors to tell his mother all his adventures.

"I must go to the fair to-morrow to see if the fairies have sent the goat back," said Benny. And the next day off he went. Sure enough, the goat was there—but will you believe it, the gnome had forgotten to make it small again, and it was simply enormous!

The Chinaman was *so* astonished! He couldn't make it out at all.

"It is a velly strange thing!" he said, over and over again. "Who can tell me what has happened?"

Benny told him—but he needn't have bothered, for the Chinaman didn't believe a word of his story! He took his enchanted goat away after the fair was over, and as far as I know, nobody has ever heard of him since.

A Puppy in Fairyland

CHIPS was a round, fat little puppy. He belonged to Alan, Jim and Betty, and they were all very fond of him. He was rather naughty, because he *would* chew slippers up, and dig great holes in the garden.

"He's a dear little chap," said Alan, "but I do wish he'd stop digging in the garden. The gardener is getting so cross!"

"Let's take him for a walk," said Betty. "If we make him tired out, he will go to sleep in his basket, and won't get into any more mischief."

So they called Chips, and he came bounding up to them, delighted to think that he was going for a walk.

"Where shall we go?" asked Alan.

"Through Heyho Wood," said Jim. "It's such a hot day, and it will be nice and cool there."

So off they started. It *was* hot! The sun shone down, and there was not a cloud in the sky. They were glad to get into the shady wood.

Chips ran here and there, sniffing at the ground in great excitement. He could smell rabbits! Then he saw one! Oh, my goodness, what a to-do there was! He yelped and barked, and tore off as fast as his short legs would let him, tripping and tumbling over blackberry brambles as he went!

"Chips! Chips! Come here, you'll get lost!" cried Alan. But Chips took no notice at all. On he went, bounding through the trees, his little tail wagging like mad. He must catch that rabbit, he really must!

But of course he didn't! The rabbit went diving headlong into its hole, and when Chips came up and looked round there was no bunny to be seen!

"It must have gone into the ground like worms do!" thought the puppy. So he chose a nice green place, and began to dig. He scrabbled the earth with his front paws, and sent it flying out behind him with his back ones. He puffed and panted, snorted and sneezed, and he took no notice at all of the shouts and whistles of the children some distance away.

Suddenly there came a shout of rage. Chips looked up in surprise, and what did he see but a brownie, dressed in a brown tunic, long stockings and a pointed hat! He was staring at Chips with a very angry look on his face, and the puppy wondered why. He didn't wonder long, because he suddenly remembered the rabbit again, and once more began to dig madly.

That made the brownie crosser than ever. He took a long green whistle from his pocket and blew seven short blasts on it. Immediately a crowd of little men like himself came up.

"Look!" said the first brownie, fiercely. "Look at that horrid dog! He's dug a hole right in the very middle of the fairy ring which we got ready for the Queen's dance to-night! And he won't stop, either!'

"Stop! Stop, you naughty dog!" cried all the brownies. "Stop digging at once."

But Chips took no notice at all. He just went on digging. The brownies didn't know *what* to do.

"He may bite if we go too near him," said one. "But we *must* catch him and punish him. Why, the Queen won't be able to have her midnight dance to-night!"

"I know how we can get him!" cried a small brownie. "Let's go and ask the spiders to give us some of their web! Then we'll throw it round the dog and catch him like that!"

"That's a good idea!" cried all the little men. "Then we'll take him to prison."

Chips looked up. He thought the brownies looked very cross indeed. He decided that he would go and find the children. But the brownies had closed round him in a ring, and he could see no way to get through. Then two or three of them came running up with a large net made of sticky spider thread. They suddenly threw it over the puppy—and poor Chips was caught!

He tried to get out of the web, but he couldn't. The brownies dragged him away, and he yelped miserably. The children heard him yelping, and looked at one another.

"Chips is in trouble!" said Betty. "Quick, come and see what's the matter!"

The three children ran as fast as they could to where they heard the puppy yelping. But when they got there, there was no Chips to be seen. There was only a cross-looking brownie filling in a newly dug hole.

"Oh!" said the children in surprise, and stopped to look at the funny little man. He looked at them, too, and then went on with his work.

"I suppose you haven't seen our puppy, have you?" asked Betty, at last.

"Oh, so it was *your* dog, was it!" said the brownie. "Well, do you know what he has done? Do you see this ring of fine green grass, surrounded by toad-stools? It was got ready for a dance to-night, by order of the Queen—and your horrid little dog dug a great big hole in the middle of it. It's all spoilt!"

"Oh dear, I *am* sorry," said Alan. "He really *is* naughty to do that—but I'm sure he didn't mean any harm. He's only a puppy, you know. He's not four months old yet."

"Well, he's been taken to prison," said the brownie. "He wouldn't even stop when we told him to!"

Betty began to cry. She couldn't bear to think of poor little Chips being taken to prison. Alan put his arm round her.

"Don't worry, Betty," he said. "We'll find some way of rescuing him."

The brownie laughed.

"Oh, no, you won't!" he said. "We shan't set him free till he's sorry."

He ran off, and disappeared between the trees. The children stared at one another in dismay.

"We *must* find Chips!" said Betty. "Where *can* they have put him?"

"Look, here are the marks of their footsteps," said Jim, pointing to where the grass was trodden down. "Let's follow their tracks as far as we can."

So they set off. Chips had been carried by the brownies, so they could find no marks of his toes, but they could easily follow the traces left on the long grass by the crowd of brownies.

Through the trees they went, keeping their eyes on the ground. Suddenly the tracks stopped.

"That's funny!" said Alan. "Where can they all have gone to? Look! they stop quite suddenly just here, in the middle of this little clearing."

"Perhaps they've flown into the air," suggested Betty.

"I don't think so," said Alan. "That little fellow we met had no wings."

"Well, did they go down through the ground, then?" wondered Jim. He looked hard at the grass and then gave a cry of excitement.

"Look!" he said. "I do believe there's a trap-door here, with grass growing neatly all over it!"

The children looked down—yes, Jim was right. There was a square patch there, which might quite well be a trap-door.

Alan knelt down, and after a few minutes he found out how to lift up the trap-door. Jim and Betty looked down the opening in excitement. They saw a tiny flight of steps leading into darkness. Alan took out his torch and flashed it into the hole.

"Look!" he cried, and picked up a white hair. "Here is one of Chip's hairs. Now we know they took him down this way! Come on!"

The three children scrambled down. There were twenty steps, and then a stone platform. To their great astonishment they saw an underground river flowing by.

"Well, Chips must have gone this way because there's no other way for him to go!" said Jim. "But how are we to follow! There's no boat to take us."

But just at that moment a little blue boat floated up, and came to the platform, where it stayed quite still.

"Hurrah!" said Alan. "Here's just what we want. Come on, you others!"

They all jumped in at once, and the little boat floated away down the dark stream. After a while it came out into the open air, and the children were very glad. They looked round them in wonder.

"This must be Fairyland!" said Betty. "Look at all the beautiful castles and palaces!"

"And look at the funny higgledy-piggledy cottages everywhere!" said Jim.

"And what a crowd of different kinds of fairy-folk!" said Alan. "Look—brownies, elves, pixies, gnomes, and lots of others!"

"I wonder where the brownies took Chips," said Betty. "Shall we ask someone and see if they know?'

"Yes," said Alan. So they stopped the boat by guiding it gently to the bank, and then asked a passing pixie if he had seen any brownies with a puppy dog.

"Yes," he said. "They had him wrapped up in spider's web, and took him to that castle over there."

He pointed to a castle nearby on a steep hill.

"Thank you," said Alan. Then he turned to the others. "Come on," he said. "We must leave this boat, and make for the castle."

Out they all jumped, and took the path that led to the castle. It was not long before they were climbing the hill on which the castle stood. They came to a great gate, and by it hung a bell-rope.

Alan pulled it, and at once a jangling noise was heard in the courtyard beyond. The gate swung open, and the children went in, feeling a little bit frightened.

There was no one in the courtyard. Exactly opposite was a door, which stood open. The children went towards it and peeped inside. Just as they got there they heard a sorrowful bark.

"Chips is here!" said Betty, in a whisper. "Let's go in."

They crept inside the door, and found themselves in a big hall. At one end was a raised platform on which stood a very grand chair, almost a throne. On it was sitting a very solemn brownie. In front of him, still tied up in the spider's thread, was poor Chips, very much afraid. Round him were scores of little brownies, and they were telling the chief one what he had done.

Betty ran right up to the solemn brownie, and Jim and Alan followed.

"Please, please let our puppy go!" begged Betty. "He didn't mean any harm to your fairy ring. He was after a rabbit, that's all."

"What sort of a rabbit?" asked the chief brownie.

"Oh, a big sandy one, with white tips to its ears," said Alan. "I saw it just as it ran away from Chips."

"Then he's a *good* puppy, not a naughty one!" cried the solemn brownie. "That rabbit is very bad. It used to draw the Queen's carriage, and what do you think it did?"

"What?" asked the three children.

"Why, one night, it *ran away* with the carriage and all!" said the brownie. "The poor Queen was so frightened. The carriage tipped over, and she was thrown out. The rabbit ran off, and we have never been able to catch it since."

"Well, Chips *nearly* caught it!" said Betty, eagerly. "And I expect he saw it go into a burrow, and tried to dig it out—only he chose the wrong place, that's all. I'm sure he's very sorry indeed for all the trouble he has caused."

"Wuff-wuff! Wuff-wuff!" said Chips, sitting up on his hind legs, and begging for mercy.

"We'll let him go at once!" cried all the brownies, and two of them ran to cut away the web that bound him. In a trice Chips was free, and danced delightedly round the three children. Betty picked him up and hugged him.

"Take them back to the wood," commanded the chief brownie. "And give Chips a bone to make up for his fright."

The puppy barked in glee when a large bone was given to him. He picked it up in his mouth and began to chew it.

"The carriage is at the door," said a little brownie, running in. The children were taken to the great door, and outside in the yard stood a grand carriage of silver and gold, driven by a brownie driver. Six small white horses drew the carriage. How excited the children were!

They all got in, said good-bye to the brownies, and then off went the carriage at a smart pace. It went up hill and down dale, through miles of Fairyland, and at last entered the same wood in which their adventures had started that morning.

"Thank you so much," said the children, as they jumped out. They patted the horses, and then the carriage turned round and was soon out of sight.

The children walked home, and told their mother all that had happened. But she found it very difficult to believe them.

"Are you sure you haven't made it all up?" she asked.

"Well, look, here is the bone that the brownies gave to Chips!" cried Betty. "And look at his tail! It's still covered with spider's web!"

So it was—and after that their mother *had* to believe their exciting story, expecially as Chips had learnt his lesson, and never, never, never dug a hole in the garden again!